Henry James: THE MAJOR PHASE

Henry James, at the age of 62

Henry James

THE MAJOR PHASE

By F. O. MATTHIESSEN

OXFORD UNIVERSITY PRESS

London   NEW YORK   *Toronto*

1944

FOR
MY INSTIGATORS,
ESPECIALLY
J.C.L.
P.T.R.
H.W.S.

Contents

Preface

THE hundredth anniversary of the birth of Henry James drew forth such a varied and fitting range of tributes that in the year after that celebration it may seem hardly useful to devote another book to him. The creative writers of my generation have recognized and assimilated his values. Auden and Spender, no matter how widely they have diverged from Eliot in politics and religion, have continued to agree with him that James is one of the few great masters of our modern literature. Practitioners of the novel who have taken its art seriously have long since responded to the high claims which Percy Lubbock made for James' technique in *The Craft of Fiction* (1921).

Yet the view of the wider public is still quite other. It is the view that—so far as American readers of history and literature are concerned—has been conditioned by Van Wyck Brooks and Parrington. Brooks' thesis, developed in *The Pilgrimage of Henry James* (1925), and not materially altered in his later evocations, is a very simple one. James was a writer of vivid and original talent who made the fatal mistake of becoming an expatriate, who thus cut himself off from the primary sources of his material, and whose works thereby lost freshness and declined until they became at last hardly more than the frustrated gestures of 'an habitually embarrassed man.' Parrington devoted two

pages to 'Henry James and The Nostalgia of Culture.' This
was one of his least happy efforts to satisfy the demands of
his publisher by making his magnificent account of the
evolution of our liberal thought seem more inclusive than
it really was, a general 'interpretation of American literature.' Far more solidly influential than Brooks' impres-
sionism, Parrington's work has been the cornerstone for
subsequent intepretations of our intellectual history. But
in the case of James, Parrington did little more than follow Brooks' lead in deploring the novelist's deracination
and cosmopolitanism. He granted some importance to his
'absorption in the stream of psychical experience,' but concluded with a sentence that reveals how far off base he
was in his demands from the novelist: 'Yet how unlike he
is to Sherwood Anderson, an authentic product of the
American consciousness!'

Such a sentence is eloquent evidence of what happens
when you divorce the study of content from form. Even
more startling conclusions can be reached when, like the
later Brooks, you neglect form and content alike, when
you merely allude to books instead of discussing and ana-
lyzing them, and reduce literary history to a pastiche of
paragraphs culled from memoirs. It is my conviction that
The Wings of the Dove searches as deeply into the American consciousness as *Winesburg, Ohio*. But in order to appreciate either book, you must be equally concerned with
what is being said and with the how and why of its saying.
The separation between form and content simply does not
exist as the mature artist contemplates his finished work.
That separation is a dangerous short-cut taken by critics,
and its disasters are written large over the history of James'

reputation. For a single symptomatic instance of the result of a critic's allowing himself to be conditioned by
such generalizations as Parrington's, Herbert Muller writes,
in his preface to *Modern Fiction: A Study in Values* (1937)
that he has 'given little attention to matters of technique,
making only a passing bow to writers like Henry James
who have brewed genteel little tempests in exquisite tea-
pots.' He would have been far more accurate in his values
if he had trusted the testimony of Edith Wharton, who had
learned from James as her chief master that: 'For him
every great novel must first of all be based on a profound
sense of moral values and then constructed with a classical
unity and economy of means.'

This last view is the one with which I also approach
James. It is a particular pleasure at this time, when the
vitality of our future culture will have to depend more
and more upon its international relations, to dwell upon
James as a forerunner of such an awareness. In diametric
opposition to Brooks and to our recent nativists in painting and the other arts, I would hold with Auden that a
modern man can hardly be said to know his own country
until he has known some other country—though such
knowledge is really an attitude of mind and does not necessarily depend on travel. I do not argue that expatriation
is either a good or a bad thing for the artist, since that
depends entirely upon the man and what he can make of
his experience. At any rate, it does not seem to have dam-
aged the work of Shelley or Ibsen or Turgenieff or count-
less brave anti-Fascist refugees of our time.

But I am not primarily concerned with James' international theme. From his first success with *Daisy Miller* that

aspect of his achievement has been the one most frequently dwelt upon. And with a writer whose work was so voluminous, it seems only sensible to take for granted the good critical work that has been done about him, and does not need to be done again. In that regard I am particularly fortunate that Joseph Warren Beach, in *The Method of Henry James* (1918), made a systematic canvass of that method under the headings of Idea, Picture, Revelation, Suspense, Point of View, Dialogue, Drama, Eliminations, Tone, Romance, and Ethics. That study still remains the best introduction to James' art, and may be supplemented by R. P. Blackmur's edition of James' own prefaces, under the title of *The Art of the Novel* (1934). A rewarding book could be written about James in terms of his relation to the evolution of the nineteenth-century novel; and such a book would find much of its spade-work done in Cornelia Pulsifer Kelley's painstaking study of *The Early Development of Henry James* (1930). Since Miss Kelley went through James' many reviews and essays about Hawthorne, George Eliot, Balzac, Turgenieff, and the other masters of fiction to whom he was indebted, and related them to all the stages of his own work up to *The Portrait of a Lady,* I have not felt it necessary to take the reader over that ground again. Moreover, the quality of the work of James' early prime has been charmingly evoked through Constance Rourke's essay on the humor in *The American*.

Profiting likewise from many other special studies, I have been able to concentrate on what interests me most, on the great works of his final maturity. Stephen Spender gave, in *The Destructive Element,* an enthusiastic account of what the modern writer can find in James, while the

darker passages of his mind, the debatable implications
of his ambiguity, have been probed—from the opposite
angles of the psychologist and the moralist—by Edmund
Wilson and Yvor Winters. Until now, however, there has
been relatively little detailed examination of his final
period as a whole, and in particular of his three major
novels, *The Ambassadors, The Wings of the Dove,* and
The Golden Bowl, and of that fourth, unfinished book,
The Ivory Tower, which gave every promise of ranking
with his best.

I agree with James' own estimate that *The Portrait of a
Lady* was his first masterpiece, but that twenty years later
with *The Ambassadors* he began to do work of a greater
depth and richness than any he had approached before.
My understanding of his development has been increased
by the rare opportunity of reading through the hundred
and fifty thousand words of his unpublished working notebooks, which, extending from 1878 to 1914, concentrate
most heavily on his aims and ambitions during the crucial
period of the eighteen-nineties.[1] The material from these
notebooks, which provided the structure for my opening
chapter, proves by itself more than ample refutation of
Brooks' whole thesis of flight, frustration, and decline.
What one sees is James' own growing consciousness of
hitherto unplumbed powers, as his first anxious and tenta-
tive hopes yield to the finally assured confidence of the
master craftsman that he is going to realize his potentialities to the full. The notebooks show that he had his first
ideas for his three crowning works eight to a dozen years

[1] An edition of these notebooks is being prepared by Kenneth B.
Murdock and myself.

before their completion; and the pursuit of those ideas to their created embodiment has given me my subject. Aesthetic criticism, if carried far enough, inevitably becomes social criticism, since the act of perception extends through the work of art to its milieu. In scrutinizing James' major novels I have tried also to write an essay in cultural history, by showing the kind of light that such novels throw back upon their time.

To preserve the singleness and wholeness of my subject I have had to turn away from certain by-paths, which I regret. Probably enough has been said in the last few years about the merits of *The Turn of the Screw,* but the whole question of James' handling of the ghost story could make an interesting chapter. I have myself tried elsewhere to see what could be discerned of James' self-portrait of the artist by treating as a group his short stories dealing with the creative life.[2] Neither *The Bostonians* nor *The Princess Casamassima* is one of James' complete successes, but treated together they could show his curious excursion into the Dickens kind of social novel, and could reveal also the strange mixture of perception and blindness in his grasp of political issues. Another omission, which I would have regretted far more, has been avoided by smuggling into an Appendix an evaluation of *The Portrait of a Lady,* in the light of James' revisions. That essay, though falling outside my main theme, is relevant to it, since through examining what James was after in revising his earlier work, we see another aspect of his final period.

As I was nearing my conclusion, a distinguished pro-

[2] In the preface to *Stories of Artists and Writers by Henry James* (New Directions, 1944).

fessor asked me what I was doing, and forgetting that he was uneasy with any literature since Trollope, I told him, only to be asked: 'What are you going to call it? *The Old Pretender?*' I had forgotten that once bright, if long since hoary, wisecrack, but that conversation gave me my title. I realized more clearly than before that though James' later evolution had involved the loss of an engaging lightness, he knew what he was about, and that if we want to find the figure in his carpet, we must search for it primarily in the intricate and fascinating designs of his final and major phase.

ACKNOWLEDGMENTS

MY first obligations are to Mr. Henry James, the nephew of the novelist, who has given his uncle's notebooks and letters to the Houghton Library at Harvard; and to the officers of that library, who have permitted me to use this material. The substance of my book was delivered as the Alexander Lectures at the University of Toronto in the fall of 1944, and I am very grateful for the opportunity that was thus provided to discuss an international theme in a country whose cultural bonds with our own will, I trust, become ever stronger.

The frontispiece is the work of Kathrine E. McClellan who, as the photographer for Smith College, took this picture for the occasion when James lectured there on 'The Lesson of Balzac,' in the spring of 1905. I want to thank Newton Arvin and Mrs. Grierson, the librarian of Smith

College, for bringing it to my attention, since it represents James during the period with which I am most concerned, at the height of his development, and gives a fine impression of both sensitiveness and strength.

I have borrowed several passages from my essay on 'Henry James and the Plastic Arts,' which appeared in *The Kenyon Review* (Autumn 1943); and the Appendix is virtually a reprint from *The American Bookman* (Winter 1944).

Every student of James is indebted, at all stages of his research, to LeRoy Phillips' admirably meticulous bibliography. My other debts extend again to the friends who have read or heard my manuscript, to C. L. Barber, Theodore Spencer, and Mark Schorer. I undoubtedly owe even more than the great amount of which I am conscious to Harry Levin's comprehensive knowledge of the novel. It is often impossible for me to tell where my ideas leave off and his begin. But I owe still more to a group of Harvard undergraduates who, during the tense winters of 1942 and 1943, kept insisting that until they were needed by the Army, they meant to continue to get the best education they could. Wiser than many of their elders, they refused to be distracted from primary values. When I said, half meaning it, that a book on Henry James was to be my overaged contribution to the war effort, they urged me to be serious. They believed that in a total war the preservation of art and thought should be a leading aim. They persuaded me to continue to believe it.

F. O. M.

Kittery, Maine

Henry James: THE MAJOR PHASE

The Art of Reflection

EIGHTEEN NINETY-FIVE was the great turning point of James' career. He was fifty-two, and his one moment of wide popularity, as the author of *Daisy Miller,* lay almost twenty years behind him. *The Portrait of a Lady* (1881) had been moderately successful, but his next two novels, *The Bostonians* and *The Princess Casamassima,* for both of which he had cherished high hopes, had almost served, as he wrote Howells, to reduce the demand for his productions to zero. Even while engaged with *The Tragic Muse* (1890), he had announced that it was to be his 'last long novel,' and though he still proposed to do short stories—'a multitude of pictures of my time, projecting my small circular frame upon as many different spots as possible'—he was soon to believe that he had found his 'real form' in the play. That illusion was to persist for five years, until the crashing failure of *Guy Domville.*

We can follow now, as we have not heretofore been able to, the course of James' hopes and intentions, as he recorded them in his notebooks. When he had returned to America in the autumn of 1881, after his first half-dozen years of continuous residence in Europe, he had declared that he had 'lost too much by losing, or rather by not having acquired, the note-taking habit. It might be a great profit to me; and now that I am older, that I have more time, that the labour of writing is less onerous to me, and I can work more at my leisure, I ought to endeavour to keep, to a certain extent, a record of passing impressions, of all that comes, that goes, that I see, and feel, and observe.' He felt particularly 'the need of summing up': 'I have done it little in the past, but it will be a good thing to do it more in the future.'

The impression conveyed by these initial pages of self-assessment is a curious one. As James runs over the chief events of his European experience, we cannot help thinking of the intellectual vacuity that had so distressed him in what he called the 'often trivial chronicle' of Hawthorne's notebooks. James is incisive enough on what he conceives to have been the main decision of his career, the decision to live in Europe. Six years have reinforced him in the rightness of that choice for his temperament and talents. He sees it not as an escape but as his assumption of the peculiar burden of being an American writer: 'The burden is necessarily greater for an American—for he *must* deal, more or less, even if only by implication, with Europe, whereas no European is obliged to deal in the least with America. No one ever dreams of calling him less complete for not doing so'—though as James looked ahead, he conjectured that 'a hundred years hence—fifty years hence perhaps' the European painter of cultures would have to reckon with our civilization as well.

But once James turns from such a penetrating generalization to the notation of what he remembers, he gives us, for the most part, a picture of the empty social world of the tourist. From his first brief stay in London he recalls only how few visits he paid. The following winter in Paris was

more rewarding, for though he had hated the new boule-
vards and hadn't managed to escape the detestable American 'set,' still he had become an habitué of the Comédie
Française, and had made the acquaintance of Turgenieff,
'most delightful and lovable of men,' and of Flaubert, 'a
powerful, serious, melancholy, manly, deeply corrupted,
yet not corrupting, nature.' But he saw that he would be
destined to remain 'an eternal outsider,' and decided then
to make his residence in London.

The odd thing about his account of his life there is that
it shows him hardly less an outsider. For page after page
he might well be any fastidious but amiable young American with a sufficient bank account to allow him to give his
time to somewhat vague cultural pursuits. He enumerates
the country houses where he stayed, and how the season
soon became a 'terror'; how 'the club question' became
'serious and difficult,' since one must have a club if one
was to remain in London; and how finally the Atheneum
proved 'an unspeakable blessing.' He found many other
advantages for a bachelor, in contrast with the interruptions of New York, where ladies invited one to call before
lunch. To be sure, he could draw up 'a tremendous list of
reasons' why London too 'should be insupportable': 'the
fogs, the smoke, the dirt, the darkness, the wet, the dis-
tances, the ugliness, the brutal life of the place, the horrible manners of society . . . You may call it dreary, heavy,
stupid, dull, inhuman, vulgar at heart and tiresome in
form.' But for 'the artist'—the word comes almost as a
shock in this context—for 'one who has the passion for observation and whose business is the study of human life,'
it is the most rewarding place in the world.

On the evidence of his notebooks you might well question how much of the city he saw, but *The Princess Casamassima* shows that he missed little, even of its submerged and desperate poverty. The same split between apparent emptiness of experience and what he could make of it—the split that has bothered nearly every critic of James—can be read in the one outline he gives of his usual day, not in London but in Venice: 'I went out in the morning—first to Florian's, to breakfast; then to my bath, at the Stabilimento Chitarin, then I wandered about, looking at pictures, street life &c, till noon, when I went for my real breakfast to the Café Inadri. After this I went home and worked till six o'clock—or sometimes only till five. In the latter case I had time for an hour or two in gondola before dinner. The evenings I strolled about, went to Florian's, listened to the music in the Piazza, and two or three nights a week went to Mrs. Brown's.' Nearly every glimpse of his personal life, in his letters as well, is just as decorous and mild, quite separated from the real concerns of any community. Not at any point in his 'summing up' is there a sign of a major intellectual or emotional event, or of any intense human relationship, save in the moving pages which describe the death of his mother. Arnold Bennett doubted whether James 'ever felt a passion, except for literature.' Yet James himself, looking back to his youth and its years of uncertainty and physical suffering, could dwell most on their 'freshness of impression and desire, the hope, the curiosity, the vivacity, the sense of richness and mystery of the world that lies before us . . . Never was an ingenuous youth more passionately and yet more patiently eager for what life might bring.' And the book he was working on, after drifting over to Venice from Nice and Mentone in 'the genial society' of two ladies, was not some mildly scented travel sketches, but the poignantly mature *Portrait of a Lady*.

A like discrepancy between means and ends might strike the further reader of James' notebooks, which, after this 'summing up,' consist, year after year, mainly of his first record of ideas for his stories. These came to him most frequently through conversations with ladies at dinner. A typical short entry reads: 'Note here next (no time today) the 2 things old Lady Stanley told me the other day that the former Lady Holland had said to her, & the admirable subject suggested to me yesterday, Sunday, at Mrs. Jennes' by Mrs. Lyon Binton's (& Mrs. J's) talk about F. H.: the man marrying for money to serve him for a great political career & public ends.' Or it is Mrs. Anstruther-Thompson, at Lady Lindsay's, telling him about a son who has sued his mother for his property. The most usual topics are the marriages, the liaisons, and the divorces of the rich, and as we reconstruct the scene and envisage the dark serious man inclining his head gravely now to the right, then to the left, we can hardly fail to be struck with how far he has drifted from the social world of his inheritance. Both his father and his elder brother were militantly democratic, and both reacted strongly against such occasions as made Henry's nightly fare, and carried away a sense of the hideous and overpowering stultification of a society based upon such class distinctions. Occasionally, after years of this society, Henry indicates that he understood what his kinsmen meant, as when something that Lady Tweedmouth said, in the mid-nineties, about 'the insane frenzy of futile occupation' suggested to him that 'a "subject" may very well reside in some picture of this overwhelming, self-defeating chaos or cataclysm toward which the whole thing is drifting.'

If many of his entries seem to show him a docile recorder of surfaces, that quickens our interest for any signs of how he went about to transmute so much idle gossip into the very different texture of his fiction. He made several solemn dedications to his art. He declared, while working on *The Bostonians,* 'A *mighty will,* there is nothing but that! The integrity of one's will, purpose, faith!' It is grotesque to find that such a resolution sprang from nothing more formidable than the need to escape from house parties. But as we come upon other such declarations in equally odd contexts, we are forced to recognize that James was himself like the aspirant to fiction whom he advised to 'try to be one of the people upon whom nothing is lost.' He was able to make much out of little. Sometimes, in these communings with himself, more relaxed than any of his published work, we seem to stumble upon the most artificial verbiage, as when he says: 'O art, art, what difficulties are like thine; and, at the same time, what consolation and encouragements, also, are like thine? Without this, for me, the world would be, indeed, a howling desert.' But no matter how much this language may sound like that of a belated dilettante of the romantic movement, we must not be fooled by it. James knew precisely what he meant, and he meant important things. For when he states, 'One does nothing of value in art or literature unless one has some general ideas,' we recognize that, like Poe, James was one of the few Americans to have grasped the truth that practice cannot be separated 'from the theory which includes it.' And he knew that theory must continually be tested by the 'frequent, fruitful, intimate battle with the particular idea, with the subject, the possibility, the place.' It was out of long years of both theory and practice that he wrote, just before undertaking *The Tragic Muse:* 'Here I sit: impatient to work, only wanting to concentrate myself, to keep at it: full of ideas, full of ambition, full of capacity —as I believe. Sometimes the discouragements, however, seem greater than anything else—the delays, the interruptions, the *éparpillement* &c. But courage, courage, and forward, forward. If one must generalize, that is the only generalization. There is an immensity to be done, and, without being presumptuous, I shall at the worst do part of it. But all one's manhood must be at one's side.'

The most fertile period to follow through his notebooks, the period of his most crucial decisions, is that inaugurated by his dramatic years. He had long wanted to work for the stage. Indeed, in his 'summing up,' he had described such work as 'the most cherished of all my projects.' He believed that he had mastered the French theater and that he knew what he was after, but he had been slow in finding the right opening. Only at the end of the eighties, when Edward Compton asked him for an acting version of *The American,* did he resolve upon the sustained experiment of writing several plays. He was completely aware of the unfavorable omens, of 'the vulgarity, the brutality, the baseness of the condition of the English-speaking theater today.' But he was eager to respond to the challenge: 'To take what there *is,* and do it without waiting forever in vain for the preconceived—to dig deep into the actual and get something out of *that*—this doubtless is the right way to live.'

But despite all his effort, his plays were a failure, not merely on the stage but in themselves. William James believed that he knew the reason: Henry had drifted in his surroundings so far from 'the vital facts of human character' that he could hardly hope to project dramatic tensions. The inertness in form, so surprising to find in James, seems due most to his determination to meet existing conditions half way, a compromise that gained him nothing and that destroyed the tight structure which had come to distinguish all his fiction.

He was never to regret having made this experiment, which bore the most valuable consequences for his later development. Despite the appearances that misled his brother, he had never flagged in his desire for fresh experience, and now the chance of working with a theatrical company had given him a renewed sense of 'all the big suggestive, swarming world around me, with all its life and motion—in which I only need to dip my ladle.' But he knew that he 'must dip with a free and vigorous hand.' He resolutely dedicated himself anew to 'the terrible law of the artist—the law of fructification, of fertilization, the law by which everything is grist to his mill—the law, in most, of the acceptance of all experience, of all suffering, of all life, of all suggestion and sensation and illumination.'

In the midst of the delays and disappointments of the theater, he found a release by dipping also 'into the *other* ink—the sacred fluid of fiction.' During these years he produced some of his best short pieces. As he said, 'the dimensions don't matter—one must cultivate one's garden. To do

many and do them perfect: that is the refuge, the asylum.'
The harvest included *The Real Thing, The Middle Years,
The Coxon Fund,* and several other stories dealing with
the problems of the creative life, *The Altar of the Dead,*
and *Owen Wingrave,* James' one story to treat the theme
of war, an eloquent denunciation of its brutality. During
these years he also kept growing in his conviction of the
supreme importance of subject. The more he saw, the more
intensely it came home to him that subjects of 'solidity,'
of 'emotional capacity' were 'the only thing on which,
henceforth, it is of the slightest use for me to expend myself. Everything else breaks down, collapses, turns thin,
turns poor, turns wretched—betrays one miserably. Only
the fine, the large, the human, the natural, the fundamental, the passionate things.'

The discrepancy is again wide between such a declaration and many of his first sketches of possible themes. For
instance, a typical anecdote that he set down in the fall
of 1892 would not seem to promise many of the abundant
attributes to which he was aspiring. It was the situation
'suggested by something lately told one about a simulta-
neous marriage, in Paris (or only "engagement," as yet, I
believe) of a father and a daughter—an only daughter. The
daughter—American of course—is engaged to a young Englishman, and the father, a widower and still youngish, has
sought in marriage at exactly the same time an American
girl of very much the same age as his daughter. Say he has
done it to console himself in his abandonment—to make
up for the loss of the daughter, to whom he has been devoted. I see a little tale, *n'est-ce pas?* in the idea that all
shall have married, as arranged, with this characteristic

consequence—that the daughter fails to hold the affections of the young English husband, whose approximate mother-in-law the pretty young second wife of the father will now have become.'

As he goes on to outline the possibilities in this compli-cation of the international marriage, envisaging that the son-in-law might be French, but that the others are all to be 'intensely American,' what seems uppermost is a me-chanically manipulated structure. The only suggestion of how such a theme might yield, not just 'a little tale,' but one of his longest novels, comes through some further re-marks on how he believed he could arrive at great subjects. 'It all comes back to the old, old lesson—that of the art of *reflection*. When I practice it the whole field is lighted up—I feel again the multitudinous pressure of all human situations and pictures, the surge and pressure of *life*. All passions, all combinations, are there.' The most intent re-flection conceivable on every ramification of this special theme was to end, a dozen years later, in *The Golden Bowl*. 'Reflection,' as James was aware, was only a shorthand sug-gestion of an intricate process. He expressed himself more comprehensively in another entry: 'To live *in* the world of creation—to get into it and stay in it—to frequent it and haunt it—to *think* intensely and fruitfully—to woo combi-nations and inspirations into being by a depth and conti-nuity of attention and meditation—this is the only thing.'

Only occasionally does one of his themes seem richly hu-man in its very first sketching. He began a fresh notebook in the fall of 1894 with several pages on the subject that was to prove his most rewarding. 'Isn't perhaps something to be made of the idea that came to me some time ago and that I have not hitherto made any note of—the little idea of the situation of some young creature (it seems to me preferably a woman, but of this I'm not sure) who, at 20, on the threshold of a life that has seemed boundless, is suddenly condemned to death (by consumption, heart disease, or whatever) by the voice of the physician? She learns that she has but a short time to live, and she rebels, she is terrified, she cries out in her anguish, her tragic young despair. She is in love with life, her dreams of it have been immense, and she clings to it with passion, with supplication.' The 'emotional capacity' of this subject is at once manifest, even though James is by no means sure yet of the details of his plot, and is thinking that he may make it into a three-act play, 'with the main part for a young actress.' Shortly after this he became involved with the rehearsals for *Guy Domville,* the only one of the five original plays he had now written that reached the stage; and there are only two or three further entries during the balance of this year.

He confronted himself with his play's catastrophic reception, at the opening of the new year, in characteristic fashion: 'I take up my *own* old pen again—the pen of all my old unforgettable efforts and sacred struggles. To myself—to-day—I need say no more. Large and full and high the future still opens. It is now indeed that I may do the work of my life. And I will.'

What follows is the most revelatory sequence in all his notebooks. In the face of adversity he is filled with an abundance of new projects. The first he sets down is an ironic comment on his own situation: 'The idea of the poor man, the artist, the man of letters, who all his life is trying—if only to get a living—to do something *vulgar,* to take the measure of the huge flat foot of the public: isn't there a little story in it, possibly, if one can animate it with an action? . . . It is suggested to me really by all the little backward memories of one's own frustrated ambition—in particular by its having just come back to me how, already twenty years ago, when I was in Paris writing letters to the *N. Y. Tribune,* Whitelaw Reid wrote to me to ask me virtually *that*—to make 'em baser and paltrier, to make them as vulgar as he could, to make them, as he called it, more "personal." Twenty years ago and so it has been ever, till the other night . . . the première of *Guy Domville.*' What sprang from that idea was no exercise in self-pity but a wryly comic story, *The Next Time,* whose novelist-hero Ralph Limbert is another example of the impossibility of making 'a sow's ear out of a silk purse.'

As James reflected further on his own disastrous bid to reach the theater public, he dwelt not on what he had lost but on what he had gained. He became aware that what he calls 'the divine principle of the Scenario' had taught him an immense amount for his fiction, especially for the clarification and tightening up of his plots. And so, instead of being oppressed by frustration, he experienced an enormous upsurge of vitality. He felt as though he had been released at last into his own proper work, since he saw more exactly than ever before what he wanted to do. Hardly a month after the collapse of his hopes for the theater he was writing: 'I have my head, thank God, full of visions. One has never too many—one has never enough. Ah, just to let one's self go—at last: to surrender one's self to what through all the long years one has (quite heroi-

cally, I think) hoped for and waited for—the mere potential and relative increase of quantity in the material act—
act of appreciation and production. One has prayed and
hoped and waited, in a word, to be able to work *more*.
And now, toward the end, it seems, within its limits, to
have come. That is all I ask. Nothing else in the world. I
bow down to Fate, equally in submission and in gratitude.
This time it's gratitude; but the form of the gratitude, to
be real and adequate, must be large and confident action—
splendid and supreme creation.'

Here we can have the rare sense of witnessing a moment
of creative inception. For the very next entry starts: 'I have
been reading over the long note—the first in this book—I
made sometime since on the subject of the dying girl who
wants to live—to live and love; and am greatly struck with
all it contains. It is there, the story; strongly, richly there;
a thing surely of great potential interest and beauty and of
a strong firm artistic *ossature*. It is *full*—this scheme; and
one has only to stir it up *à pleines mains*.'

He then turns to another possibility by which he has
been haunted, that of doing a new short 'international
novel,' since Harper has urged him to return to the theme
of his earlier days. He thinks that something probably lies
there, if he will only give it time to emerge. 'Meanwhile
in my path stands—appears at least to stand—brightly so-
liciting, the idea I jotted down a year ago, or more, and
that has lain there untouched ever since: the idea of the
father and daughter (in Paris, supposedly) who marry—
the father for consolation—at the same time, and yet are
left more together than ever, through their respective
époux taking such a fancy to each other. This has many

of the very elements required: it is intensely international, it is brief, dramatic, ironic &; and this mere touching of it already makes my fingers itch for it. I seem to see in it something compact, *charpenté,* living, touching, amusing. *Everything* about it qualifies it for Harper except the subject—or rather, I mean, except the adulterine element *in* the subject. But may it not be simply a question of *handling* that? For God's sake let me try: I want to plunge into it: I *languish* so to get at an immediate creation.'

That particular act of creation was not to be fulfilled until nine years later. But at this moment, with the themes for *The Wings of the Dove* and *The Golden Bowl* both in his mind, he arrived at his most elaborated formulation of what he had salvaged from his bitter experience of working for the stage. '*If* there has lurked in the central core of it this exquisite truth—I almost hold my breath with suspense as I try to formulate it; so much, so *much,* hangs radiantly there as depending on it—this exquisite truth that what I call the divine principle in question is a key that, working in the same *general* way fits the complicated chambers of *both* the dramatic and the narrative lock: *if,* I say, I have crept round through long apparent barrenness, through suffering and sadness intolerable to that rare perception—why my infinite little loss is converted into an almost infinite little gain.' He soared even higher in his effort to find sufficiently exquisite words for the 'magicality' of his discovery that he might draw on the method of the play for his fiction. But he knew that proof was everything, that how much value there really was for his stories in 'the close, clear, full scenario' could only be told by trying.

The first trial he was to carry through, of *nouvelle*

length, was on a theme he had noted down two years before, of the struggle over property between a mother and
son. But even while he was engaged with *The Spoils of
Poynton,* in the autumn of 1895, he was struck with the
anecdote that was to provide him with the subject for *The
Ambassadors,* the anecdote that Jonathan Sturges had told
him about a short and interrupted visit that Howells had
recently made to Paris. Called home unexpectedly by an
illness in his family, he had laid his hand on Sturges' shoul-
der and said: 'Oh, you are young, you are young—be glad
of it: be glad of it and *live.* Live all you can: it's a mistake
not to . . .' Even as James started to amplify this speech,
it suggested 'a little structure.' Just as with the theme for
The Golden Bowl, he seemed at first to see here 'something of a tiny kind.' He was preoccupied at this time with
economy, with perfecting the short form. To be sure, no
piece of his fiction seems ever to have turned out as short
as he hoped, and presently he is worrying that *Poynton,*
planned as a story of ten thousand words, has grown to
more than three times that length. But though he fears
that means that the *Atlantic* will not want it, nothing can
dampen his spirits, nor diminish the sense of creative
abundance with which he is swelling at the close of this
year. Just to keep track of the subjects that have occurred
to him as possible for novels, he makes a list of a dozen, of
which the first two items are:

La Mourante: the girl who is dying, the young man and
the girl he is engaged to.

The Marriages (what a pity I've used that name!): the
Father and Daughter, with the husband of the one and the

wife of the other entangled in a mutual passion, an intrigue.

He was actually to start next on *What Maisie Knew*, always keeping several shorter things on the fire. With each renewal of effort, he reaffirmed what the drama had taught him for his own method. He advised himself that the structure of *Poynton* 'must be as straight as a play—that is the only way to do. Ah, *mon bon*, make this, here, justify, crown, in its little degree, the long years and pains, the acquired mastery of scenic presentation.' While absorbed in working out its sequence of scenes he was led to hope that he had gained at last the 'mastery of fundamental statement.' The intricate problem of consciousness with which he faced himself in treating Maisie made him want to work out with special care 'a really detailed scenario,' an 'intensely structural, intensely hinged and jointed preliminary frame.' In every case he recognized the futility of loose generalizations about art. The only thing of value was the fresh and particular experiment.

He was to carry farthest his experiments with direct dramatic technique in *The Awkward Age*, where virtually the entire novel has been restricted to dialogue. Throughout the last half of the nineties he also continued to recur to the potentialities of 'the very short thing,' to the merits of 'the single incident.' Then, in the last winter of the century, his emphasis shifted. He had just come down to Rye, filled, after some weeks in London, with 'the old reviving ache of desire to get back to work.' What first tempted him, as he sat in his 'little warm white study' listening to the perpetual winter gale, was a possible renewed attempt at a short play, 'the divine little difficult, artistic, ingenious, architectural form that makes old pulses throb . . .' But within a week he had changed his direction. He was thinking once more of the novel, and wrote: 'How, through all hesitations and conflicts and worries . . . the desire to get back only to the *big* (scenic constructions, "architectural" effects) seizes me and carries me off my feet making me feel that it's a far deeper economy of time to sink, at *any* moment, into the evocation and ciphering out of *that*, than into any other *small* beguilement at all. Ah, once more, to let myself go!'

The tone of that aspiration takes us back to the final entry in his notebook of 'summing up' so many years before. He had been berating himself for his vagueness of mind, for his wretched habits 'of work and of un-work,' for his repeated failure to focus his attention: 'I shall be 40 years old in April next: it's a horrible fact! I believe, however, that I have learned how to work and that it is in moments of forced idleness, almost alone, that these melancholy reflections seize me. When I'm really at work, I'm happy, I feel strong, I see many opportunities ahead. It is the only thing that makes life endurable. I must make some great efforts during the next few years, however, if I wish not to have been on the whole a failure. I shall have been a failure unless I do something *great*.'

II

'The Ambassadors'

'THE AMBASSADORS,' the first of James' three crowning
works to be completed,[1] has proved by far his most popular
book with the critics. In this they have followed his lead,
since he announced in the preface that it was 'frankly, quite
the best, "all round,"' of all his productions. He wrote it
with gusto, declaring to Howells as he felt his way into its
composition in the summer of 1900, that it was 'human,
dramatic, international, exquisitely "pure," exquisitely
everything . . . My genius, I may even say, absolutely
thrives.' Such fresh confidence carried into the texture of
the book. After the strained virtuosity of *The Awkward*

---

[1] *The Wings of the Dove* appeared in 1902, *The Ambassadors* not
until 1903. But *The Ambassadors* had been finished by the summer
of 1901, and this reversal of the order in which they were written
was caused by its acceptance for serialization in *The North American
Review* (January-December, 1903).

One application that James had made of what he had learned
through his plays of the art of the Scenario was in his long preliminary sketches or 'projects' for both these novels. He referred to these
sketches, in a letter to Wells (November, 1902), as being exceptional
to his former practice, and said that the one for *The Ambassadors* ran
to twenty thousand words, that for *The Wings* to only half such
length. He added that he had destroyed the latter. The former he
had submitted to Harper's as the basis for serialization, and believed
to have been destroyed by them. But it was rescued from their files
and published, in part, by Edna Kenton in the James number of
The Hound and Horn (Spring 1934). If there was a comparable
scenario for *The Golden Bowl,* it presumably has also been destroyed.

Age and *The Sacred Fount,* James expanded into a theme that was both opulent and robust. He expressed the mood that had been phrased by Longfellow's brother-in-law Tom Appleton: 'All good Americans, when they die, go to Paris.' Appleton was talking of the era directly after the Civil War, the era James had recorded in *The American.* But the mood was to persist, and for the next post-war period, for the generation of the nineteen-twenties, Paris was still the same 'huge iridescent' jewel it was for Strether, the symbol of liberation from every starved inadequate background into life.

What caused James' preference for the book was not its theme, but its roundness of structure. On the same grounds of ' "architectural" competence' his second favorite was *The Portrait of a Lady.* In *The Ambassadors* we have a fine instance of the experienced artist taking an external convention, and, instead of letting it act as a handicap, turning it to his own signal advantage. James had always been uneasy—as well he might have been!—with his age's demand for serialized fiction. But here for once he felt a great stimulus to his ingenuity, and he laid out his novel organically in twelve books, each of which could serve for a month's installment. His subject was well fitted to such treatment, since it consisted in Strether's gradual initiation into a world of new values, and a series of small climaxes could therefore best articulate this hero's successive discoveries. It is interesting to note also the suspense that James creates by the device of the delayed introduction of the chief characters in Strether's drama.

The opening book at Chester, where Strether, arriving from Liverpool to meet his friend Waymarsh, encounters

first Maria Gostrey, is really a prologue that strikes the
theme of Europe—the Europe of old houses and crooked
streets which was also being stamped upon American im-
aginations by James' contemporary, Whistler. The second
book begins in London, and though Strether is already
started on his eager growth through fresh impressions, how
far he still has to go is indicated by Maria's remark that
the theater which he takes 'for—comparatively—divine' is
'impossible, if you really want to know.' During this conversation Chad Newsome's name is first casually introduced, and then followed by expertly swift exposition of
the situation which Strether has come out to rectify. But
we don't see Chad himself for some time yet. Strether must
have his initial taste of Paris, that 'vast bright Babylon.'
And as he stands in the Boulevard Malesherbes looking
up at the balcony of Chad's apartment, he recognizes in a
flash, in the essence of Jamesian revelation, that the life
which goes on in such balanced and measured surroundings cannot possibly be the crude dissipation that Woollett,
Massachusetts, believes. His initiation has reached its crucial stage.

Only at the end of this third book does Chad himself
appear, with a dramatic entrance into the back of Maria's
and Strether's box at the Comédie. In a neat instance of
how he could meet the devices of the serial, James has him
sit there through the darkness of the act, with Strether intensely conscious of his presence; and brings the two of
them face to face in conversation not until after the play,
at the beginning of book four. In that book Strether tact-
fully feels his way into friendship with Chad; and in the
next he is introduced to Madame de Vionnet. It is signifi-

cant that the declaration for life which was the seed of this novel flowers into its full form, as spoken by Strether to Little Bilham, immediately after this introduction. The next two books concentrate on Strether's developing relationship with Madame de Vionnet, from his first call on her to his boldly flouting Woollett and taking her out to lunch. Before the end of this book, a little more than half way through the novel, his position and Chad's are reversed: Chad says he is willing to go home and it is Strether who now urges him to stay.

Such conduct brings its swift retribution, with the arrival, in book eight, of the new ambassador, Mrs. Newsome's formidable daughter Sarah Pocock, who has been sent to take over the duties of the wavering Strether. The portrait of the Pococks—Sarah, Jim, and Mamie—is one of James' triumphs in light-handed satire, in the manner he had mastered in *Daisy Miller* and had developed further in that lesser known but delightful *jeu d'esprit, The Reverberator*. With the Pococks the cast is finally complete, and it is an astonishing tribute to James' skill that the most intensely realized presence in the novel is that of Mrs. Newsome, who never appears at all and yet looms massively like 'some particularly large iceberg in a cool blue northern sea.'

The critical point in book nine is the announcement that Madame de Vionnet's daughter is to be married, which leaves Strether, blind until now to the actual situation, with the growing awareness that it must be Madame de Vionnet herself to whom Chad is somehow bound. The tenth book moves rapidly to Sarah's being outraged at what she regards as Strether's treachery to her mother, and to her ultimatum that her entourage is leaving Paris. The eleventh book rises to the most effective climax of all, Strether's glimpse of Chad and Madame de Vionnet together on the river, and his long-delayed perception of their real relationship. What is left for the concluding book is his final interview with Madame de Vionnet, which James was inclined to regard as the novel's 'most beautiful and interesting' scene. Then, after a last talk with Chad, Strether faces with Maria what the whole experience has come to mean for him.

What most concerned James in this structure was also his principal contribution to the art of the novel, his development in Strether of a center of consciousness. What Strether *sees* is the entire content, and James thus perfected a device both for framing and for interpreting experience. All art must give the effect of putting a frame around its subject, in the sense that it must select a significant design, and, by concentrating upon it, thus empower us to share in the essence without being distracted by irrelevant details. James' device serves greatly to reinforce such concentration, since if every detail must be observed and analysed by Strether, we obtain a heightened singleness of vision. We obtain both 'the large unity' and 'the grace of intensity' which James held to be the final criteria for a novel. His contribution here has been fully assessed by critics, and has been assimilated in varying degrees by many subsequent novelists. Indeed, some have gone so far as to declare *The Ambassadors* the most skillfully planned novel ever written. The chief reminder we need now is that there is a vast difference between James' method and that of the novels of 'the stream of consciousness.' That phrase was used by William James in his *Principles of Psychology,* but in his brother's novels there is none of the welling up of the darkly subconscious life that has characterized the novel since Freud. James' novels are strictly novels of intelligence rather than of full consciousness; and in commenting on the focus of attention that he had achieved through Strether, he warned against 'the terrible *fluidity* of self-revelation.'

What James saw in Strether was what made him want to write the novel, as his long notebook entry of 1895 had elaborated. The idea that had come to him first was that of 'an elderly man who hasn't lived, hasn't at all, in the sense of sensations, passions, impulses, pleasures . . . He has never really enjoyed—he has lived only for duty and conscience . . . lived for effort, for surrender, abstention, sacrifice.' James had begun at once to imagine the possibilities. He shied away at first from having the revelation come to his hero in Paris, on the grounds of being too expected and banal. He wasn't absolutely certain that the man should be American: 'he might be an Englishman.' But as James went on to conceive the putative histories of men who had not lived, his hero's background became unmistakable: 'I can't make him a novelist—too like W. D. H. and too generally *invraisemblable.* But I want him "intellectual," I want him fine, clever, literary almost: it deepens the irony, the tragedy. A clergyman is too obvious and *usé* and otherwise impossible. A journalist, a lawyer—these men *would* in a manner have "lived," through their contact with life, with the complications and turpitudes and general vitality of mankind. A doctor—an artist too. A mere man of business—he's possible; but not of the intellectual grain that I mean. The Editor of a Magazine—that would come nearest: not at all of a newspaper. A Professor in a college would imply some knowledge of the lives of the young—though there might be a tragic effect in his seeing at the last that he hasn't even suspected what these lives might contain. They have passed by him—he had passed them by.'

The austerity and aloofness of the still unnamed Strether have by now determined him as unquestionably a New Englander. One aspect of his situation that James projected in his notebook outline but did not use in the book was that his hero's blindness to passion should have caused him in the past to have misunderstood and so to have sacrificed some wild son or younger brother. But now all the sources of emotion, all the 'influences and appeals' he had not reckoned with are to be brought home to him. James hit directly upon the situation he was to use, that of his hero's having come to Europe to bring back some young man whose family are anxious. 'The idea of the tale,' as he summed it up, was to consist then in 'the revolution that takes place in the poor man' as he ranges himself unexpectedly *du côté du jeune homme.'* James has already conceived what sacrifice that will mean for his hero, that he will lose 'the strenuous widow,' whom he was to have married, 'and all the advantages attaching to her.' 'It is too late, too late *now* for *him* to live—but what stirs in him with a dumb passion of desire, of I don't know what, is the sense that he may have a little supersensual hour in the vicarious freedom of another.' The signal omission from this outline is any mention of Madame de Vionnet. The transformation of that phrase, "of I don't know what,' into the richest source of Strether's awakening is one token of how much James' final themes accrued by the years in which he let his imagination play over them before bringing them to completion.

The challenge to *live,* in its short initial form, had dwelt solely on the elderly man's warning—James stipulated his age as fifty-five—against the repetition of his mistake. James' immense elaboration of this challenge tells how much it meant to him. As Strether delivers it in Gloriani's garden, it becomes in fact the quintessential expression of a dominant theme that runs throughout James' work. A whole succession of his heroes and heroines had been possessed with the same desire. Roderick Hudson's thirst for experience had been so violent that it had hurtled him to destruction; but for Christopher Newman, who had retired from business in early middle life, and for Isabel Archer, just on the threshold of her twenties, there had seemed every possibility for the abundance Strether had missed. All these characters were Americans for whom the symbol of abundance had been Europe, but a similar eagerness for liberation was to seize upon some of James' European heroes—notably Hyacinth Robinson (of *The Princess Casamassima*), who was finally crushed by the class divisions that had kept him from his desire, and Nick Dormer (of *The Tragic Muse*), who had turned his back on a political career to live more intensely in the practice of art. Such is the recurrent pattern of James' novels, and the same theme could be followed through any number of his short stories, from the frustrated aspirations of Clement Searle, 'the passionate pilgrim' (1871), down to the tragedy of the spiritual emptiness of John Marcher, in *The Beast in the Jungle* (1903), whose lot it was to have been the man 'to whom nothing whatever was to happen.'

Strether introduces into his version of this declaration for life a highly complex image, which serves to reveal his Puritan heritage. It is the image of life as a tin mould, be it plain or fluted and embossed, into which the 'helpless jelly' of one's consciousness is poured by 'the great cook.' In this way Strether symbolizes the illusion of free will: the form of the individual consciousness has been prede-termined and limited, not, to be sure, by the Puritans' God, but by every force in the individual's background and envi-ronment. Yet Strether insists that we make the most of life by enjoying our illusion, that we should act as though we were free. James had already shown his concern with such a philosophical theme in *The Portrait of a Lady*. Isabel Archer, a daughter of the transcendental enlightenment, was confident that the world lay all before her, that she could make whatever fine choice she liked. James knew how wrong she was in that belief, and demonstrated that her every act was determined by the innocence, the willful eagerness, the generous but romantic blindness to evil that she had derived from her nineteenth-century American conditioning.

James himself did not have the heritage of American Puritanism. He spoke of his not being a New Englander 'as a danger after all escaped.' He remarked also, 'Boston is absolutely nothing to me—I don't even dislike it.' But to understand all the overtones with which he charged the imperative *live,* we must remember that his grandfather was an Irish Presbyterian. Against that background James' father was in revolt. Yet even as he responded to Emerson's rejection of the old restrictions, he found that philosopher dangerously limited by his refusal to reckon with Calvinism 'as a fact at all' in his sublime superiority to evil. Most of Henry James Senior's own declarations, as he ripened into his version of Swedenborgianism, were on the side of optimism and expansion. In that he proved himself a child of his age, but the strong residue of his concern with the nature of evil was to be transmitted to his sons, though ultimately more to the brooding novelist than to the hopeful philosopher.

Yet Strether's declaration, except for its qualifying of free will, continues, essentially, the transcendental mood of liberation. What had proved so heartening to Emerson's contemporaries was his insistence that life for Americans no longer needed to be starved. The most intense expression of that conviction, perhaps the most intense single passage in American writing, is Thoreau's development of a theme extraordinarily like Strether's. When Thoreau declared why he went to the woods, he too revealed the depth of the New England dread that a man might die without ever having lived. But Thoreau's will was in dynamic response to the challenge, and he expressed his desire 'to suck out all the marrow of life' in a series of physical images, the energy of which was quite beyond Strether—or James.

The relative attenuation of Strether's desire, its passive rather than active scope, is one of the most striking consequences of James' own peculiar conditioning. No experimental child of the nineteenth century, not even John Stuart Mill, was brought up more deliberately on a theory. That theory, as James described it in *Notes of a Son and Brother*, sprang from his father's profound aversion to the narrow competitive drives of American life. What he wanted for his sons was the greatest possible range of spiritual experience—'spiritual,' as Henry noted, was his father's 'most living' word—before they should be limited by the dictates of a career. In fact, as Henry was humorously aware, his father carried his dread of their being circumscribed to such lengths as to deplore their decision upon any career at all, and continued in the hope that they were instead 'just to *be* something, something unconnected with specific doing, something free and uncommitted . . .'

Such a theory could have resulted in utter dispersion in a group with less passion for ideas than the James family possessed. But as it affected both the older boys, it induced a slow but richer ripening. It may well have caused some of William's early nervous tensions, as he struggled to find himself by turning from painting to experimental science to medicine, and only finally to psychology and philosophy. But it meant that when he finally wrote his first book, at the age of forty-seven, in the same year as Henry's *Tragic Muse,* he produced a masterpiece, *The Principles of Psychology.* Henry's tensions were less apparent but extremely acute, and the more glimpses we catch of them, the more we perceive why a declaration like Strether's spoke so much for himself as well. On the verge of manhood, the injury to his back that kept him from participating in the Civil War made him feel that his was the peculiar case of having to live inwardly at a time of 'immense and prolonged outwardness.' For many years thereafter his health continued to be so precarious that he was afraid he might never be able to bring his expression of life to the fullness for which he longed, an anxiety which found its way into such a story of an artist's frustration as *The Madonna of the Future*. As he came through to middle age, he began to find stability, and though in his 'summing up' he could recall that his twenties had been 'a time of suffering so keen that that fact might seem to pin its dark colours to the whole period,' nevertheless the dominant strain in his memories was quite other. He could feel at last the satisfaction of having 'wanted to do very much what I have done, and success, if I may say so, now stretches back a tender hand to its younger brother, desire.'

But he was still to have many hours of his old anxiety, of feeling merely on the verge of completion. And though, unlike Strether, he had not been shut out from the opportunity for impressions of life, still he was to come back again and again to a central dilemma. He made his most complete declaration of it shortly after he had started to work for the stage. His advice to himself should be put beside Strether's advice to Bilham: 'The upshot of all such reflections is that I have only to let myself *go*. So I have said to myself all my life—so I said to myself in the far-off days of my fermenting and passionate youth. Yet I have never fully done it. The taste of it—of the need of it—rolls over me at times with commanding force: it seems the formula of my salvation, of what remains to me of a future. I am in full possession of accumulated resources—I have only to use them, to insist, to persist, to do something more,—to do much more,—than I *have* done. The way to do it—to affirm one's self *sur la fin*—is to strike as many notes, deep, full, and rapid, as one can. All life is—at my age, with all one's artistic soul the record of it—in one's

pocket, as it were. Go on, my boy, and strike hard; have a rich and long St. Martin's Summer. Try everything, do everything, render everything—be an artist, be distinguished to the last.'

Another decade was to elapse before he was able to let himself go to his full extent, and to say finally the most that he had to say. His Saint Martin's summer really began with *The Ambassadors*. It is notable that the two New England minds of his own generation with whom he had most enjoyed friendship during his Boston years were to come to equally late flowering. Henry Adams was not to write his *Mont-Saint-Michel and Chartres* until he was past sixty-five and his *Education* until he was almost seventy. Wendell Holmes was to arrive at his full stature only after he reached the Supreme Court, at sixty-one, in the same year as *The Ambassadors* appeared. These other late harvests, along with those of the James brothers, are evidence against the current belief that American talents always burn themselves out after an early promise. They may indicate too that the older New England strain could come to valuable expression, in the period of New England's cultural decline, only if it had the stamina to survive its arid surroundings and so mature at last the rich juices for which Adams in particular felt himself parched.

What Strether awakened to in Paris was not unlike the aesthetic experience that Adams came finally to know only as he discovered the beauty of the cathedrals. Strether keeps emphasizing the importance of seeing, and we know that James himself lived in large measure by his eyes. He developed very early the feeling that intense life concentrated itself into scenes of which he was the absorbed spectator. This was to mean that of the two types into which Yeats divides artists, those who, like Blake, celebrate their own immediate share in the energy that 'is eternal delight,' and those who, like Keats, give us a poignant sense of being separated from what they present, James belonged to the latter. He described his own early romantic longing for 'otherness' in terms very close to those Yeats was to use for Keats:

I see a schoolboy when I think of him,
With face and nose pressed to a sweet shop window . . .

James said that in his childhood 'to *be* other, other almost anyhow, seemed as good as the probable taste of the bright compound wistfully watched in the confectioner's window, unattainable, impossible . . .' His account too of the kind of delight he took in his first 'pedestrian gaping' along Broadway delineates even more sharply the type to which he belonged. For at this very same time, in the early eighteen-fifties, an incipient American poet had also been drinking in the sights of this same street. But Whitman was to make his poetry out of passionate identification with everything he saw, not out of detachment. James, on the other hand, came to believe that 'the only form of riot or revel' his temperament would ever know would be that 'of the visiting mind,' and that he could attain the longed for 'otherness' of the world outside himself only by imaginative projection which, by framing his vision, could give it permanence.

What Strether sees is what James saw, the Europe of the tourist. But James conceived of seeing in a multiple sense, as an act of the inward even more than of the outward eye. An interesting chapter of cultural history could be written about the nineteenth century's stress on sight. When Emerson declared that 'the age is ocular,' and delighted in the fact that the poet is the seer, he was overwhelmingly concerned with the spiritual and not the material vision. But concern with the external world came to mark every phase of the century's increasing closeness of observation, whether in such scientific achievements as the lenses for the telescope and the microscope, or in the painters' new experiments with light, or in the determination of the photographers and the realistic novelists to record every specific surface detail. Matthew Arnold was to note that 'curiosity' had a good sense in French, but unfortunately only a bad one in English. James, an early convert to Arnold's culture, set himself to prove the value of the farthest reaches of curiosity. The distance that he had travelled from Emerson may be measured by the fact that though both knew their chief subject matter to be consciousness, the mind's awareness of its processes, for Emerson that awareness reaffirmed primarily the moral laws. James was also a moralist, but aesthetic experience was primary for him, since ἀισθητικός meant perceptive. He had turned that double-edged word 'seer' back to this world. As he said in the preface to *The Ambassadors*, 'art deals with what we see, it must first contribute full-handed that ingredient; it plucks its material, otherwise expressed, in the garden of life—which material elsewhere grown is stale and uneatable.' But what distinguished him from French naturalists and English aesthetes alike was that he never forgot the further kind of seeing, the transcendent passage to the world behind appearance and beyond the senses.

Emerson had exulted that the eye was 'the best of painters,' but his poetry and prose were both woefully lacking
in plastic quality. James deliberately cultivated the skills
of the painter. The first form he had experimented with
as a small boy was what he called in his reminiscences 'dramatic, accompanied by pictorial composition,' short scenes
each followed by its illustration. At the time when William
was working in Hunt's studio, Henry at seventeen had
shown his own shy curiosity in sketching. And although
he soon realized that he had no talent, and turned to fiction, 'it was to feel, with reassurance, that the picture was
still in essence one's aim.' He was to continue to train his
eye by means of his long series of 'portraits of places,'
wherein he followed the lead of Gautier and other French-
men who were bringing literature closer to the art of the
Impressionists. He was finally to arrive at the explicit
statement that he wanted such a story as *The Coxon Fund*
to be 'an Impression—as one of Sargent's pictures is an impression.'

The perfected instance of his belief that the novelist
should 'catch the colour of life' is the way he initiates
both Strether and the reader into Paris. His accuracy of
presentation is such that he can really suggest the quality
of Chad's existence through the very look of his house, 'its
cold fair grey, warmed and polished a little by life.' James
makes such a magnificently functional use of his architectural details that his hero is persuaded—and thousands of
his countrymen have had the same yearning belief—that
the life which goes on behind those windows and that balcony must also be characterized by tact and taste, by 'the
fine relation of part to part and space to space.' And when

Strether throws to the winds all scruples as to what Mrs. Newsome would think, and invites Madame de Vionnet to lunch, James presents us with a fully achieved canvas: 'How could he wish it to be lucid for others, for any one, that he, for the hour, saw reasons enough in the mere way the bright clean ordered water-side life came in at the open window?—the mere way Madame de Vionnet, opposite him over their intensely white table-linen, their *omelette aux tomates,* their bottle of straw-colored Chablis, thanked him for everything almost with the smile of a child, while her grey eyes moved in and out of their talk, back to the quarter of the warm spring air, in which early summer had already begun to throb, and then back again to his face and their human questions.'

Here he has come to the essence, not of Sargent's effects but of Renoir's, in the wonderful sense of open air; in the sensuous relish of all the surfaces, with exactly the right central spot of color in that *omelette aux tomates;* in the exquisite play of light around his figures. And when James added a further accent, it made for the very kind of charm by which the Impressionists declared their art a release from stuffy manners as well as from stale techniques: Madame de Vionnet 'was a woman who, between courses, could be graceful with her elbows on the table. It was a posture unknown to Mrs. Newsome . . .'

James' cities, unlike Balzac's or Joyce's, focus on the inviting vistas presented to the well-to-do visitor. The very air of Strether's Paris has the taste 'of something mixed with art, something that presented nature as a white-capped master-chef.' But James was not ignorant of what he called 'the huge collective life' going on beyond his charmed circle; and at the end, when Strether is meditating on Madame de Vionnet's suffering, he thinks too of the vast suffering Paris has witnessed, and senses in the streets their long ineradicable 'smell of revolution, the smell of the public temper—or perhaps simply the smell of blood.' Yet such omens are black shadows looming only at the very edge of James' pictures. What he chose to frame, specially selected though it is, takes on an intensity to the degree that he could realize the multiple kinds of seeing in which he had striven to perfect himself, and could demonstrate that he had mastered 'the art of reflection' in both senses of that phrase—both as a projector of the luminous surfaces of life, and as an interpreter of their significance. Perhaps the most brilliant instance of this double skill in all James' work is the recognition scene on the river, a scene which reveals also his extraordinary awareness of how art frames experience. He took great delight in adapting plastic devices for a highly developed, wholly unexpected illustration of this aesthetic process.

When Strether decides on a day in the country, what leads him there is his far-off memory 'of a certain small Lambinet that had charmed him, long years before, at a Boston dealer's.' It is interesting to recall that this nearly forgotten painter of scenes along the Seine was of the era of Rousseau and Daubigny, all of whom James noted as having been first shown to him in the early days by Hunt.

On one plane, Strether's being drawn by art to nature to verify an old impression, shows the curious reversal of order in the modern sensibility. On another plane, as he dwells on how much that canvas, not expensive but far beyond his purse, had meant to him in the Tremont Street gallery, we have a sharp contrast between Strether's New England actuality and his long smothered French ideal. But James doesn't leave it at that. Strether's entire day progresses as though he had 'not once overstepped the oblong gilt frame.' The whole scene was there, the clustered houses and the poplars and the willows: 'it was Tremont Street, it was France, it was Lambinet.' In the late afternoon, as he sits at a village café overlooking a reach of the river, his landscape takes on a further interest. It becomes a Landscape with Figures, as a boat appears around the bend, a man rowing, a lady with a pink parasol. There, in an instant, was 'the lie in the charming affair.' The skill with which James has held our eyes within his frame has so heightened the significance of every slight detail that such a recognition scene leaps out with the force of the strongest drama.

What Strether has seen comes to him as a great shock, but it does not cause him to waver in his judgment of how much Chad has improved. What he is anxious about now is whether Chad is really worthy of what Madame de Vionnet has given him, and there are plenty of undeveloped hints at the close that he is not, that he is already restive, that he will not be happy permanently without the business world, and that he may even soon be turning to a younger woman. What then finally is the positive content of Strether's challenge to Bilham? As far as that young painter is concerned, the possibilities seem very slight. His eye has taken in so much of the beautiful surface of Paris that his productive power has faltered before it; and though he is happy with his vision, his is certainly a mild version of the doctrine of being rather than of doing.

What then of Strether himself, what has he gained from his initiation? Waymarsh warned him at the outset that he was 'a very attractive man,' and Maria Gostrey says that he owes more to women than any man she ever saw. Yet when he encounters Gloriani, Strether is acutely conscious of his own 'rather grey interior.' He expresses his sense of the Italian sculptor's vitality through an image of the sexual jungle: he both admires and envies 'the glossy male tiger, magnificently marked.' How far James himself had advanced in his penetration into character may be instanced by his different handling of this same Gloriani in *Roderick Hudson* nearly thirty years before. There the worldly sculptor had been somewhat cheap in his sophistication as he played the rôle of a Mephistopheles to Roderick's Faust. But now James suggests an unfathomable depth of 'human expertness' in his eyes, an enormous fund of 'terrible' energy behind his smile.

It is revelatory of the careful pattern that James worked out in *The Ambassadors* to note the sequence of events in this crucial scene in Gloriani's garden. As he first takes in the beauty of his surroundings in the heart of the Faubourg Saint-Germain, Strether reflects to Bilham: 'You've all of you here so much visual sense that you've somehow all "run" to it. There are moments when it strikes one that you haven't any other.' Almost at once thereafter Strether is presented to Madame de Vionnet, and when she moves on after a few moments' conversation, he faces Bilham with his declaration for life. This, in turn, he follows with his expressed envy of Gloriani. None of these connections are made explicit, a sign that James' way of creating Madame de Vionnet's charm is to render it more pervasive in its operation than anything he says about it. Before the close of this scene he remarks that Strether is the kind of man who receives 'an amount of experience out of any proportion to his adventures.' That, we recall, is what James also rejoiced over in his preface, that in Strether he had had his full chance 'to "do" a man of imagination.'

But what does Strether finally make of his experience? The issue at the close shows how rigorously James believed that an author should hold to his structure. He had posited his hero's sense that it was too late for him to live; and had reinforced this with Strether's New England scrupulosity that in siding with Chad his conscience could be clear, since there was to be 'nothing in it for himself.' And no matter how bewilderingly iridescent he finds the jewel-image of Paris, since 'what seemed all surface one moment seemed all depth the next,' Strether never loses his moral sense. James seems to have taken his own special pleasure in avoiding the banal by not making Paris the usual scene of seduction but instead the center of an ethical drama. Another aspect of the structure— and its most artificial—is the rôle of *ficelle* conceived for Maria Gostrey. She exists only as a confidante for Strether, only as a means of letting him comment on his experience. Consequently, as James himself noted, she had a 'false connexion' with the plot which he had to bend his ingenuity to make appear as a real one. But his device of having her fall in love with Strether and hope wistfully to marry him does not achieve such reality.

It serves rather to exaggerate the negative content of Strether's renunciation. He has come at last, as he says, to *see* Mrs. Newsome, and we know by now how much is involved in that word. But he leaves Paris and Maria to go back to no prospect of life at all. We are confronted here with what will strike us much more forcibly in *The Golden Bowl,* the contrast in James between imputed and actual values. The burden of *The Ambassadors* is that Strether has awakened to a wholly new sense of life. Yet he does nothing at all to fulfill that sense. Therefore, fond as James is of him, we cannot help feeling his relative emptiness. At times, even, as when James describes how 'he went to Rouen with a little handbag and inordinately spent the night,' it is forced upon us that, despite James' humorous awareness of the inadequacy of his hero's adventures, neither Strether nor his creator escape a certain soft fussiness.

What gives this novel the stamina to survive the dated flavor of Strether's liberation is the quality that James admired most in Turgenieff, the ability to endow some of his characters with such vitality that they seem to take the plot into their own hands, or rather, to continue to live beyond its exigencies. The center of that vitality here is the character not reckoned with in James' initial outline. For what pervades the final passages is Strether's unacknowledged love for Madame de Vionnet. James has succeeded in making her so attractive that, quite apart from the rigid requirement of his structure, there can really be no question of Strether's caring deeply for any other woman. The means that James used to evoke her whole way of life is a supreme instance of how he went about to give concrete embodiment to his values. Just as he devoted the greatest care to the surroundings for Strether's

declaration and explicitly drew on his own memories of
the garden behind the house where Madame Récamier
had died, so he created Madame de Vionnet entirely in
terms of and inseparable from old Paris. Every distinction
in her manner is related to Strether's impression of her
house, where each chair and cabinet suggests 'some glory,
some prosperity of the First Empire, some Napoleonic
glamour, some dim lustre of the great legend.' In his 'summing up' James had attempted to convey why the great
English houses had grown to mean so much to him. It
was primarily their 'accumulations of expression': 'on the
soil over which so much has passed, and out of which so
much has come,' they 'rose before me like a series of visions . . . I thought of stories, of dramas, of all the life
of the past—of things one can hardly speak of; speak of,
I mean at the time. It is art that speaks of those things;
and the idea makes me adore her more and more.'

That gives us insight into why James, to a greater degree than any other American artist, was a spokesman for
the imagination as a conserving force. He believed that art
is the great conserver, since it alone can give permanence
to the more perishable order of society. Yet, despite the
usual view of him, James dwelt very little in the past. His
impressions and his reading were preponderantly, almost
oppressively, contemporary. His one living tap-root to the
past was through his appreciation of such an exquisite
product of tradition as Madame de Vionnet. Yet, as he
created her, she was the very essence of the aesthetic sensibility of his own day. Strether can hardly find enough
comparisons for her splendor. Her head is like that on
'an old precious medal of the Renaissance.' She is 'a god-

dess still partly engaged in a morning cloud,' or 'a sea-nymph waist-high in the summer surge.' She is so 'various and multifold' that he hardly needs to mention Cleopatra. And though Mona Lisa is not mentioned, James is evoking something very like Pater's spell. Although James' moral residues are considerably different from Pater's, both Strether and James could have subscribed to much of Pater's famous exhortation for fullness of life, particularly to the sentence which urges that one's passion should yield 'this fruit of a quickened, multiplied consciousness.'

But Madame de Vionnet is more human than Pater's evocation. On the last night that Strether sees her, she seems older, 'visibly less exempt from the touch of time.' And though she is still 'the finest and subtlest creature' he has ever met, she is, even as Shakespeare's Cleopatra, troubled like 'a maid servant crying for her young man.' In an image which enables him to fuse the qualities with which he especially wants to endow her, James makes Strether think that her dress of 'simplest coolest white' is so old fashioned 'that Madame Roland must on the scaffold have worn something like it.' Madame de Vionnet's end is also to be tragic. She has learned from life that no real happiness comes from taking: 'the only safe thing is to give.' Such a nature is far too good for Chad, and she realizes now that 'the only certainty' for the future is that she will be 'the loser in the end.' Her positive suffering and loss are far more affecting than Strether's tenuous renunciation. Why it was that James could create women of much greater emotional substance than his men we can tell best by turning to *The Wings of the Dove.*

III

'The Wings of the Dove'

'THE FIGURE IN THE CARPET' has struck many readers as an instance where James' curiosity has been anything but idle, where, indeed, it has run into the ground. All the characters in that story are so obsessed with pursuing the hidden meaning of Hugh Vereker's novels that their criticism turns into a nightmarish game as the very issues of life and death are engulfed in their excessive and finally futile ingenuity. But James' intention was much fresher than his effect. His preface tells us that he had designed virtually a fable on behalf of analytic appreciation, a plea for perception, the very secret of which was in danger of being lost altogether by the careless readers of the new mass novel of the day. And in his notebook draft James had his novelist assure the young critic that what could be likened to the complex pattern in a Persian carpet 'isn't the "esoteric meaning," as the newspapers say: it's the *only* meaning, it's the very soul and core of the work.' He spoke of it also as the 'special beauty' that had presided over his books, that had controlled and animated them.

James' fable has yielded a symbol for critics by reminding them that their task is not fulfilled unless they have passed beyond the trees to the wood, and have seen an artist's achievement in its entirety. In a more restricted but very relevant sense one may also look for the essential design, not through the successive stages of an artist's whole development, but in his masterpiece, in that single work where his characteristic emotional vibration seems deepest and where we may have the sense, therefore, that we have come to 'the very soul.

Such a book in James' canon is *The Wings of the Dove,* the animating beauty of which is its heroine, Milly Theale. James began his preface by saying that this book represented to his memory 'a very old—if I shouldn't perhaps rather say a very young—motive,' since he could scarcely remember the time when its situation had not been vividly present to him. He went into no further explanation there, but in the final chapter of his *Notes of a Son and Brother* (1914), the chapter that completed his account of William's and his own young manhood, he was to uncover the long hidden source of the threads he had tried to weave into the center of his novel. For Milly Theale, to the greatest degree that James ever based one of his characters on actual life, is his tribute to his cousin Minny Temple, who had died of tuberculosis at twenty-four. His sense of this loss, remaining at the core of his personal life and yet ramifying outward through the long years of his subsequent social experience, empowered him to create in Milly Theale the most resonant symbol for what he had to say about humanity. We may best understand James' ultimate values if we recover something of the long background of his associations before turning to their embodiment in the novel.

As he looked back to their late twenties, when William had been finding his way through acute depression to his final orientation in psychology, and when his own literary efforts had still appeared fairly vague, he remembered too the vividness, the extraordinary play of minds. Their circle had included Temples and Emmets in New York, John Lafarge and Thomas Sargent Perry from the Newport years, and John Chipman Gray as well as Wendell Holmes in Boston. He remembered the tone of their talk about Browning or about George Eliot's latest novel. But he remembered most keenly how Minny Temple had been their heroine.

His first image of her carried her back to earlier dancing days at Delmonico's. But the period he wanted to memorialize was when he had responded to her 'dancing flame of thought,' when she had struck him as possessing 'beyond any equally young creature I have known a sense for verity of character and play of life in others.' She was already under the shadow of grave illness, but was always marked by a lightness all her own, a reckless impatience of her lot, an entire lack of care for herself. When he came to evoke her quality in his autobiography, his practice of his craft had long since taught him that to recover an image is to recover its context. So he let her portray herself, for the most part, through a group of her letters to another friend, who, though James does not say so, was John Gray, later to be a distinguished judge. They are remarkably full letters, passing from personalities and discussion of the books and music she liked to brief but grim details about her hemorrhages, which she met with the belief that they could be conquered, if only her will to live was strong enough. She herself commented on the intense restlessness of her spirit; and what gives not only her own image but that of her time is her eagerness to face with her friend the whole range of belief.

James declares that she had both too much sensibility and too much irony to be charged with 'female earnestness.' But though she said that she had never studied much, she was deeply concerned to find the truth. She had found religion very difficult, since she was often bewildered by 'the indissoluble mixture of the divine and the diabolical in us all.' But she felt the necessity of some certainty about 'the meaning and end of our lives,' and in one of the intervals when she was well enough to be going about again, she turned to the sermons of Phillips Brooks, in the hope that he would be able to expound 'the old beliefs' with a clearness that would convince her and banish doubt forever. James sees it 'quaint,' in retrospect, that such urgency of question could have hoped for an answer in that 'enormous, softly massive and sociably active presence,' since the Episcopal Bishop, 'of capacious attention and comforting suggestion, was a brave worker among those who didn't too passionately press their questions and claims . . .' And presently Minny had discovered for herself that Mr. Brooks was 'all feeling and no reason,' that he was 'good for those within the pale, but not good to convince outsiders that they should come in.'

She clung to Christ's 'all-embracing humanity,' but, instead of arriving at certainty, she turned back to 'the old *human* feeling, with its beautiful pride and its striving, its despair, its mystery and its faith.' As she felt her future ever increasingly menaced, she came to the realization that 'we must each of us, after all, live out our own lives apart from everyone else.' But this realization meant no diminution in the quickness of her sympathies. She followed with anticipation all news of her friends. She said that Willy James has 'the largest heart as well as the largest head,' and 'is one of the very few people in this world that I love.' She is delighted that Harry has been able to go to Europe, and hopes that 'it will do him good and that he will enjoy himself—which he hasn't done for several years.' Harry was shortly to write back to William of his revulsion from the dowdiness of English women: 'I revolt from their dreary deathly want of—what shall I call it?—Clover Hooper has it—intellectual grace—Minny Temple has it—moral spontaneity.'

He preserved throughout life an image of his last visit to her before he had sailed. He recalled her slim fairness, her extraordinary pallor—which he had fatuously thought of as 'becoming,' the way she had tossed her head, and her laugh that had emphasized her large mouth. But though their talk had all been of gaiety in his plans for Italy, just 'as if no corner of the veil of the future had been lifted,' the impression he was to keep of her in the midst of her 'generous, gregarious' Emmet cousins was that 'of a child struggling with her ignorance in a sort of pathless desert of the genial and the casual.' She was dead by the following spring.

She had kept up her courage to the end, and had said that she had fortunately enough Irish blood in her 'rather to enjoy a good fight.' But, as James wrote on the final page of Notes of a Son and Brother, 'Death, at the last, was dreadful to her; she would have given anything to live.' She was to endure in his consciousness as 'the supreme case of a taste for life as life, as personal living.' Her image was to continue to haunt him as being 'so of the essence of tragedy' that he could say now, a dozen years after he had written *The Wings of the Dove,* that he had sought there 'to lay the ghost by wrapping it . . . in the beauty and dignity of art.'

He took deep satisfaction too in his readers' response to his effort to preserve and enshrine her in her own image. As he wrote to an old friend of them both, 'Our noble and unique . . . little Minny's name is *really* now, in the most touching way, I think, silvered over and set apart.' He said that William and he had felt her death together as the end of their youth, and that it was on William's behalf especially that he spoke. But a small sheaf of unpublished letters brings out deeper contours in the picture. Minny's first letter to him in Europe begins: 'My darling Harry (You don't mind if I am a little affectionate, now that you are so far away, do you?).' She spends most of her space regaling him with items about their friends, passing quickly over the fact that she has been very ill again, but before she closes, she adds: 'I shall miss you, my dear—but I am most happy to know that you are well and enjoying yourself. I wish I were there too. If you were not my cousin, I would write and ask you to marry me and take me with you—but as it is it wouldn't do.'

One does not have to take that declaration too earnestly, but it adds many further threads to the strong strand that bound them together. She continued to play with the idea that at least some of her family might take her to Italy to join him, but as the year wore on, she had to face the fact that her health would never permit her to go abroad. In her last letter she has heard of his being in poor health and spirits in Florence, and only hopes that his troubles are counterbalanced by some true happiness: 'I think the best comes through a blind hanging on to some conviction, never mind what, that God has put deepest into our souls, and the comforting love of a few chosen friends.'

At the news of her death James wrote immediately to his mother: 'It is no surprise to me to find that I felt for her an affection so deep as the foundations of my being, for I always knew it.' In another unpublished letter, to Charles Eliot Norton's sister Grace, who was to remain for many years a chief confidante of the hopes and fears of his career, he went on to say that he wasn't sure whether she ever knew Minny well enough to understand 'how great a sense of loss' her death brings 'to those who really knew her—as *I* did . . . Her friendship had always been for me one of the happiest certainties of the future. So much for *certainties* . . . She was a divinely restless spirit—essentially one of the "irreconcilables"; and if she had lived to great age, I think it would have been as the victim and plaything of her constant generous dreams and dissatisfactions. During the last year moreover it had become obvious that her life would be one of immense suffering—suffering far harder to think of than (to me at least) even the death which has cut short the sweetness of her youth . . . I feel not only much the wiser for having known her, but —I find—really the happier for knowing her at absolute peace and rest. Her life was a strenuous, almost passionate *question,* which my mind, at least, lacked the energy to offer the elements of an answer for.'

Ten years after her death he wove some of Minny's traits into Isabel Archer, whose story he declared to Grace

Norton 'is much the best thing I have done, though not the best I shall do.' But he added that he had not intended a portrait. 'Poor Minny was essentially incomplete—and I have attempted to make my young woman more rounded, more finished. In truth everyone in life is incomplete, and it is the mark of art that in reproducing them one feels the desire to fill them out, to justify them, as it were.' In *The Wings of the Dove* he was to cleave closer to some of the actual circumstances of Minny's case, and yet to give her some of the completion she had missed. He could scarcely be said to have given an answer to her question, but he had brought to full expression her kind of tragedy—and his.

Why it was especially his kind of tragedy might be underscored by many further details. In the first chapter of his earliest reminiscences, *A Small Boy and Others* (1913), he remarked on the impression that had been made on him by the fact that his father's family had shown so many 'dawnings' on which 'the deepening and final darknesses were so soon to follow . . . such a chronicle of early deaths, arrested careers, broken promises, orphaned children.' Minny and her five brothers and sisters had lost both their parents; and this had seemed to James' boyhood imaginings a deepened source of romance. A peculiar trait in his fiction was to be the frequency with which he presented his leading characters as bereft of any immediate family. In the case particularly of Isabel Archer and Milly Theale he seemed to feel that by making them orphans he had heightened the pathos of their encounter with destiny.

On another level, less explored by the light of his consciousness, this succession of family disasters must have increased his own feeling of insecurity. He began *The Middle Years,* his unfinished account of his mature career, with dwelling on how he had gone to Europe in that last year of Minny's life with the sense that his freedom might be brief and his experience broken, an apprehension produced by his 'having been so long gravely unwell.' It needs no amateur psychoanalyzing to read into his many declarations for life an escape from the burden of his private anxieties. At the ambivalent pole of his insecurity was a revulsion from life, no less profound for being decorously hidden from public view. When he had to write Howells about the death of his daughter at the end of the eighteen-eighties, he said: 'I can't talk of death without seeming to say too much—I think so kindly of it as compared with life—the only thing one can compare it to.' At the time when he was discussing his *Portrait of a Lady* with Grace Norton, he had also said to her: 'I am unlikely ever to marry . . . One's attitude toward marriage is a fact—the most characteristic part doubtless of one's general attitude toward life . . . If I were to marry I should be guilty in my own eyes of inconsistency—I should pretend to think quite a little better of life than I really do.'

But the pathos of early death, dramatizing the agony of both the intensity and the insecurity of life, was hardly a theme special to James. It has been a peculiarly recurrent American theme. It is startling to realize that the subject of *The Wings of the Dove* is precisely what Poe formulated as the greatest possible subject for poetry, the death of a beautiful woman. For Poe's kind of romanticism, to be sure, James had little taste, announcing, in his unsympathetic essay on Baudelaire, that an enthusiasm for

Poe's poetry was 'the mark of a decidedly primitive stage of reflection.' But the theme of deprivation, of loss, of lack of fulfillment was a characteristic product of James' milieu. Henry Adams was to symbolize the end of his youth and his first full awareness of life's brutality in the tragic death of his sister. After the loss—through suicide—of his wife, the Clover Hooper whose intellectual grace James had remarked, Adams was to devote his deepest intellectual energies to understanding the medieval cult of the Virgin; and was to endow his portrait of Her with much the same rare distinction of subtlety and refinement that James bestowed upon his heroines.

Both Adams and James grew increasingly conscious of the waning of old energies. Both looked back to an American world that had been shattered by the Civil War, a world in which the Adams family had had power, and in which the James family had been able to live in a charmed circle of leisure, happily oblivious of the rising giants of business. Neither Adams nor James could be said to have remotely understood the American world of their maturity. Adams could approach its new energies only by a brilliant but dubious analogy between the laws of history and of thermodynamics. James repeatedly confessed that the world an American Balzac would have to master—the world of industrial and finance capitalism—had been a closed book to him from his youth. Inevitably, therefore, the emotional symbols of these writers were feminine. They wrote in an elegiac spirit, and were further exemplars of the lack of male principle in our literature that Emerson had deplored. But if we read James instead of deploring him, we may be impressed that what started as a personal motive became socially, indeed almost nationally representative of a phase in our history when, whether we liked it or not, the American girl, the heiress of all the ages, was the sign by which cultivated Europe knew us.

The depth and complexity of feeling which James brought to his theme could hardly be better illustrated than by the transmutation of his notebook sketch into the completed *Wings of the Dove*. There is no indication in his three-thousand-word outline of the autumn of 1894 that he had Minny Temple in mind, and many of his initial details would promise little more than the usual society novel. He thought of the scene as being 'at Nice or Mentone—or Cairo—or Corfu'; but he also struck frankly to the source of vitality, noting that the 'something' which it breaks the girl's heart to die without having known 'can only be—of course—the chance to love and to be loved.' But as he reflected on the problem presented by the girl's illness, he was bothered by the idea 'of physical possession.' Such a remedy for her despair seemed incongruous, even ugly, under the circumstances. ' "Oh, she's dying without having it? Give it to her and let her die" '—that struck him 'as sufficiently second-rate.' He knew that if he were writing for a French public, 'the whole thing would be simpler—the elder, the "other" woman would be simply the mistress of the young man, and it would be a question of his taking on the dying girl for a time—having a temporary liaison with her.' But he believed that one could 'do so little with English adultery': it was 'so much less inevitable, and so much more ugly in all its hiding and lying side,' since it was 'undermined by our immemorial tradition of original freedom of choice.'

The aspect of the situation that he began to think his way into—and he used his notebooks as a means of catching his thoughts as they rose—was the particular attitude of the man. The 'disinterestedness of his conduct' was to lie in the fact that though he pitied the girl deeply, he was not in love with her, even though she was in love with him. At this point James arrived at the crucial temptation: both the man and his fiancée were to be without money, while the dying girl was rich. He dropped his notes here and came back to them a few days later with the thought that he could scarely imagine any denouement that wasn't 'ugly and vulgar.' Then he got hold of the idea of making 'that happiness, that life, that snatched experience the girl longs for *be,* in fact, some rapturous act . . . some act of generosity, of passionate benefice, of pure sacrifice to the man she loves.' Thereupon he began also to put the initiative for the plan to get the money upon the fiancée instead of upon the man, and also posited that the two girls were not to 'love each other.'

As the plot began to balance and enmesh, he conceived that he might make it into a play, but he wanted no such happy ending as the current stage demanded. For the girl was to die, but even after discovering the secret engagement between the others, she was still to leave a great deal of money to the man she had 'so hopelessly and generously loved.' He, in turn, was to have conceived a horror for the scheme in which he had become involved, and 'in the light of how exquisite the dead girl was, he sees how little exquisite is the living.' There is to be 'a very painful, almost violent scene between them . . . They break, in a word, . . . as the woman gives him, in her resentment and jeal-

ousy (of the other's memory, now), an opening to break—by
offering to let him off. But he offers her the money and she
takes it. Then, vindictively, in spite, with the money . . .
she marries Lord X, while he lives poor and single and
faithful—faithful to the image of the dead.' Only in the
final sentences of this outline did James see his heroine
'perhaps as an American.'

In the eight years between this sketch and the published
novel that 'perhaps' was to become a leading motive. In fact,
the extreme and peculiar liberty with which he wanted to
endow his heroine, 'liberty of action, of choice, of appreciation, of contact,' could, as he perceived in his preface, best
be that of the inordinately rich New York heiress with all
the world at her feet. Against that dazzling freedom was
to be arrayed an inexorable fate, the uncontrollable force
of her illness. But though she is 'stricken and doomed,' she
is not to be presented as infirm. Indeed, the tension of the
drama must rise from her passionate eagerness for life,
from the vivid helpless courage with which she combats
her doom. Here, especially, Minny Temple's qualities became those of the heroine. Here also was the source of the
emotional vibration with which James was finally most
concerned. As he wrote to Howells, who had asked him for
another 'terror' story like his recent *Turn of the Screw,*
he was so preoccupied 'with half a dozen things of the altogether human order' now fermenting in his brain that
he didn't care any longer 'for "terror" ("terror," that is,
without "pity").' He was then at work on *The Ambassadors,* which was to give scope to pity but scarcely to terror. His most effective combination of the two was in *The
Wings of the Dove.*

James, who tended to discuss his finished works solely in terms of their realized form, was not satisfied with this book. He wrote to Howells that it was 'too long-winded'; to another friend, that it had 'too big a head for its body,' or, speaking more exactly, that its center wasn't 'in the middle.' What he meant by this notion of the misplaced middle he developed in his preface, as he had previously done in that to *The Tragic Muse*. He believed that he had fallen into too great amplitude in his opening treatment of Kate Croy against her family background. This fault, as he wrote to Wells, might have been the result of the fact that, to his disappointment, his plans for serialization had failed (' . . . evidently no fiction of mine can or *will* now be serialized'); and he had gone ahead and developed his scenario 'on a more free and independent scale.' Whatever the cause, he had devoted so much initial space to Kate and Densher that when he had come to his main theme he had had to foreshorten mercilessly, and was afraid that in the last half in particular he had been too crowded, and had produced 'the illusion of mass without the illusion of extent.'

The reader may be inclined to agree, and certainly there is not the symmetrical structure which James achieved in both *The Ambassadors* and *The Golden Bowl*. But the characterizing feature in the method of *The Wings of the Dove*, to which James' preface scarcely does justice, is its deliberately *indirect* presentation of its heroine. The very nature of the theme, involving the fact that Milly is essentially the sufferer rather than the actor, makes it imaginatively right that she should seem surrounded by the others, and that, at the close, because of her illness, she should have been long off stage. That does not mean that her final image is any the less intense, as the ordonnance of the ten books can show.

The first two are given over entirely to Kate and Merton Densher. Milly is not even mentioned, but the London world and the particular situation into which she is to be projected are presented with impressive solidness. The short third book tells us what we need of Milly's background, and brings her to Europe with Susan Shepherd Stringham, a lady writer from Boston who plays the rôle of the Jamesian confidante. The next book introduces them to England, and, through Susan's having formerly known Kate's Aunt Maud Lowder, directly into the circle of their complications. The fifth book, which, without the restrictions of the serial, can become much longer, embraces the whole swift course of Milly's social triumph in London; and though James thought that his foreshortening here had still made his action pivot too rapidly, no passage in all his work gives us more of the felt splendor of life. The sixth book sets in motion Kate's scheme of Densher's being 'kind' to Milly; and the seventh, where the scene changes to Venice, is the last to center around the heroine. In the eighth she makes her final public appearance, at an evening party for her friends, where her frail form is silhouetted against the glamorous setting she is so soon to lose. Thereafter we see her only once more, in a conversation with Densher, in which she voices her last passionate declaration of wanting so much to live, just before Lord Mark turns up with his brutal news that Kate and Densher have been engaged all the time. This news smashes her delicate hold on life, and it was James' instinct that the way to handle such a denouement was entirely without big scenes. The reader of other fiction may feel cheated that he gets at first hand neither her talk with Lord Mark nor her final interview with Densher, in which she forgives him. But James' device of having his heroine not appear during the last fifth of the novel—just as she had not in the opening sections—and of having the final book in London record her death far away in Venice, succeeds extraordinarily in making us feel as though Milly has been wrapped around and isolated by sinister forces, almost as though she has been literally smothered off stage by Kate's terrifying will.

His detailed treatment of Kate at the outset, no matter how much it may have interfered with later proportions, had been absolutely necessary if he was to account for her character and conduct. She is by no means the nakedly brutal villainness that he had projected in his notebook. She is a much more living mixture of good and evil, a far more effective register of James' mature vision of human complexity. She is handsome, she has immense vitality, and she is without resources. Moreover, her selfish family—her sister who frets in the squalor of her lower-middle-class marriage, her father who has been involved in unspecified shady dealings—expect her to do well by them. She is aware that material things speak strongly to her also, and, to help her family's situation and her own, she has gone to live with her wealthy and ambitious aunt. Kate recognizes that Aunt Maud is 'unscrupulous and immoral'; she knows that she has been accepted into the house only as a potential social asset who must make an important marriage—and she has fallen in love with Merton Densher, a young jour-

nalist with no more money than she has. The importance
of wealth had not been ignored in *The Ambassadors:* as
Strether declared, it was 'the root of the evil' in his difficult situation with Mrs. Newsome. But Strether's heart was
not set on money, and even without Mrs. Newsome's, he
would not be really poor; whereas for Kate, once she is
tempted, desire for money becomes the great corrupter.

James makes an incisive contrast between Kate and
Densher. He specifies that they have little in common except their affection, that Densher tends to be as passive as
Kate is active, that her talent is all for life and his for
thought. Indeed, James has created here, somewhat more
affectingly than in Strether, the kind of hero which our
age has associated with the sensibility of the metaphysical
poets, one whose 'remembered thoughts . . . at the moment of their coming to him had thrilled him almost like
adventures.' They face together the impossibility of their
situation: as Kate says, they are 'hideously intelligent' in
the lucidity with which they see that their secret engagement cannot look for sympathy from any quarter. But
James does not scant the strength or the beauty of their
attachment. To those inattentive critics who keep insisting
that James is always flinching from physical passion, the
final pages of book two, just before Densher leaves for a
special assignment in America, should be ample refutation.

The contrast which James develops between Kate and
Milly is one of quantity against quality, of blood against
nerves, of robust health against haggard delicacy. It is sustained through every detail of their appearance. Kate's
striking handsomeness depends on clearness of eye and
skin, on the regularity of her features, on the smooth dis-

tinction of her social charm. Milly's pallor makes her hair seem exceptionally red, while her large irregular nose and mouth could allow her to be called beautiful only by those who are attracted by 'American intensity.' It may be an accidental residue of romanticism that, as was the usual practice of Hawthorne and Melville, the innocent heroine is fair, and the dangerous worldly girl is dark.

But the more one scrutinizes the technique of this novel, the more one perceives that, despite James' past-masterly command over the details of realistic presentation, he is evoking essentially the mood of a fairy tale. He wanted to raise his international theme to its ultimate potentiality. He was no longer satisfied to endow an Isabel Archer with a legacy sufficient to allow her to confront Europe independently. He was bent on extending the sources of his splendor to the farthest conceivable degree. Milly was to be a fabulous millionairess. He deliberately wove an atmosphere of enchantment around her by the device of having Susan Stringham regard her as a 'princess.' Susan herself makes the comparison between them as that between 'the potential heiress of all the ages' and 'a mere typical subscriber . . . to the *Transcript.*' But Susan's imagination has been fed on Pater and Maeterlinck. Hers is explicitly the Puritan imagination 'finally disencumbered' of its background and determined to make up for all its 'starved generations' by discovering in Milly the richest possibilities of romance. Even the girl's utter loss 'of parents, brothers, sisters' can be construed by Susan as 'all on a scale and with a sweep that required the greater stage; it was a New York legend of affecting, of romantic isolation . . .' With such a confidante for interpreter and chorus, James can introduce even fairy-tale imagery without its seeming forced or out of tone. The open sesame by which Susan's earlier friendship with Aunt Maud brings them at once to the heart of the London season is playfully likened by Milly to the wand of a fairy godmother; and in this brilliant new world of dinner parties which, in an echo from *The Tempest*, Milly finds 'rich and strange,' she feels as though she is sustained by 'an Eastern carpet.'

This would seem an appropriate occasion to consider the particular rôle played by imagery in James' writing, since, with his later books, as indicated by such titles as *The Sacred Fount, The Wings of the Dove, The Golden Bowl, The Ivory Tower,* images have become so important that they have passed over into symbols. Moreover, the use of images in *The Wings of the Dove* is so functional that we may keep our discussion of them integrally related to the rest of our discussion of this novel.

At the opening of his autobiographical memoirs James was to declare that the only terms in which life had treated him to experience were 'in the vivid image and the very scene.' He had been demonstrating the accuracy of that formulation from the time of his earliest stories. His first sign of unmistakable distinction was his rapid mastery of the skills of concrete presentation. He had schooled himself assiduously in the realistic novelists, but his own special gift was the product of his trained eye and of his intensely pictorial imagination. The animation of his early style most frequently was owing to the clarity of his perceptions. This picture of old Mr. Touchett on his deathbed is a good example of what he had mastered at the time of writing

The Portrait of a Lady: 'Something of that veiled acuteness with which it had been, on Daniel Touchett's part, the habit of a lifetime to listen to a financial proposition, still lingered in the face in which the invalid had not obliterated the man of business.'

But James did not remain satisfied with such general pictures. The whole bent of his later descriptions was to make them more visually complete. This appears throughout his revisions. Where he had originally spoken of Mr. Touchett's hope that Ralph might 'carry on the bank in a pure American spirit,' he was to change it to: 'carry on the grey old bank in the white American light.' Take for another instance his introduction of Fidelia Dosson, a very American girl in *The Reverberator,* which was written at the height of his early period, in 1888: 'It was a plain, blank face, not only without movement, but with a suggestion of obstinacy in its repose; and yet, with its limitations, it was neither stupid nor displeasing. It had an air of intelligent calm—a considering, pondering look that was superior, somehow, to diffidence or anxiety; moreover, the girl had a clear skin and a gentle, dim smile.' When James reworked this twenty years later for his collected edition, he used only a few more words; but he now suggested the girl's qualities by a series of images that characterized her: 'It was a plain clean round pattern face, marked for recognition among so many only perhaps by a small figure, the sprig on a china plate, that might have denoted deep obstinacy; and yet, with its settled smoothness, it was neither stupid nor hard. It was as calm as a room kept dusted and aired for candid earnest occasions, the meeting of unanimous committees and the discussion of flourishing businesses.'[1]

By the time of his full development James had discovered the secret of even more elaborate devices, particularly that he could bind together his imaginative effects by subtly recurrent images of a thematic kind. In *The Ambassadors* he conveyed Strether's sense of the rapid flowing away of existence by leading up to his famous declaration through a passage describing the accumulating 'stream' of his impressions, their 'gathering to a head,' and their final spreading out and overwhelming him with the 'long slow rush' that he poured out to Bilham. We find similar water-images—such images for life's flux as had, incidentally, been pervasive in Emerson—at other emotional high points of Strether's career. It is twice stipulated how Madame de Vionnet is drawing him into her boat and onto the current, and as further images keep up his sense of floating along, we are being prepared for the cumulative effect of the actual scene on the river.

A similar frequency of images of floating might be noted in *The Wings of the Dove*, where the serene 'high-water mark' of Milly's London success must be contrasted with her view of 'the troubled sea' that looms ahead, with the shipwreck that may lie in store for 'the ark of her deluge.' Since the recurrent pattern of an artist's imagery is the

[1] It was in accordance with the demands of such virtuosity that James carried out his revisions. A typical change was his description of Ralph Touchett. Instead of saying that 'his face wore its pleasant perpetual smile, which perhaps suggested wit rather than achieved it,' James wrote: 'Blighted and battered, but still responsive and still ironic, his face was like a lighted lantern patched with paper and unsteadily held.' For a detailed account of James' later use of such characterizing images, see the Appendix on *The Portrait of a Lady*.

most telling evidence of how he envisages the qualities of life, another odd variant of James' water-images is worth citing. In all three of his great final novels he conceives on occasion his social group as being 'like fishes in a crystal pool,' held together in 'a fathomless medium.' What James seems to want most to suggest through such an image is the denseness of experience, the way in which the Jamesian individual feels that he is held into close contact with his special group, the slowly circulating motion of their exist-ence all open to the observing eye, and, particularly as Densher develops this image, with an oppressive sense of the complexities in which he is immersed, of being plunged into an element 'rather more strangely than agreeably warm'.

If you proceeded to enumerate and categorize all of James' leading images, as has recently been done with Shakespeare's, you would undoubtedly gain a great deal of intimate insight both into the way his imagination worked and into what it worked upon. But the author of a long novel can scarcely depend on iterative imagery to produce atmosphere to the heightened degree that a poet can in the compressed length of a play, and we may learn more about James' art by examining the function of a few of his most elaborated images than by pursuing the se-quence of their scattered and often minor echoes.

At the close of the chapter in which he introduced Milly, James wanted to sum up effectively the various and in-tricate aspects of the impression she had made upon Susan, and was designed to make upon the reader. During their brief sojourn in the Alps, Susan comes upon Milly one afternoon seated on the 'dizzy edge' of a precipice. She

stifles a cry at the danger there of 'a single false movement,' at the possible latent betrayal in Milly's caprice of
'a horrible hidden obsession.' But as she watches, she is
reassured: 'If the girl was deeply and recklessly meditating there she wasn't meditating a jump . . . She was
looking down on the kingdoms of the earth, and though
indeed that of itself might well go to the brain, it wouldn't
be with a view of renouncing them. Was she choosing
among them or did she want them all?' Through such a
pictorial image we have borne in upon us one aspect of
Milly's situation which James wants us never to forget,
that the menace of death is always near her. But as Susan
realized, Milly wouldn't try a quick escape 'from the human predicament': 'she knew herself unmistakably re-
served for some more complicated passage . . . It would
be a question of taking full in the face the whole assault
of life.' By that extension James enables us to look ahead
to his drama. He centers anticipation through Susan's consciousness of what must lie in store for a girl of Milly's
type, of 'her history, her state, her beauty, her mystery.'

One thing notably absent from such a compelling image
is any apparent awareness by James of its full religious
implications. When Hawthorne had Miriam and Donatello
reenact the fall of man, he was thoroughly conscious of
the roots of his scene in the Bible, and especially in Milton.
But James is concerned only with the beautiful sweep of
the possible kingdoms at Milly's feet. At no point in this
novel does he want to suggest that she is tempted by the
devil in her choice of this world. So, too, with James' casual introduction of an image to suggest the chief source of
Densher's attraction for Kate. This lies in the greater range

of his intellectual experience, which James expresses by
Densher's 'having tasted of the tree and being thereby prepared to assist her to eat.' All that James wants to suggest
is the tree of knowledge; he seems to have forgotten that
such an image is inescapably one of temptation, since it
is certainly not Kate who is led into evil by Densher. Such
carelessness or obliviousness on James' part shows how far
he had drifted from the firm Christian knowledge that
Hawthorne possessed, a fact that we will have to reckon
with in his curious treatment of evil in *The Golden Bowl.*

The type of image with which James is most successful
is that which allows him to draw on the whole reach of his
plastic resources. If *The House of the Seven Gables* had
originally suggested to him the device of using a portrait
to bring out character, he was to develop this device into
one of his supreme recognition scenes. On the very next
page after Milly has introduced the image of 'an Eastern
carpet,' she is brought to the peak of her enchantment. As
she is escorted by Lord Mark to see the wonderful Bronzino in the great house, which picture, as everyone agrees,
looks so like her, James has completed his spell and transformed his heroine into a Renaissance princess. By virtue
of insisting on this likeness he has caused Milly to feel that
she has entered 'the mystic circle': 'things melted together—
the beauty and the history and the facility and the splendid midsummer glow: it was a sort of magnificent maxi-
mum, the pink dawn of an apotheosis coming so curiously
soon.' But at this exalted moment Milly also foresees that
none of her happiness will last. Even as she looks, she
realizes that the joyless lady on the canvas is 'dead, dead,

dead'; and the words reverberate for us as an omen of her own future.

This scene before the Bronzino operates almost like a musical theme: it strikes the first note of the transition to Venice, where Milly plays out her make-believe rôle in the gorgeous rented palace which increases the ironic contrast 'between her fortune and her fear.' There her setting becomes explicitly a Veronese, and Susan, to whom again this comparison occurs, deems all the sumptuous magnificence to be only fitting, since Milly's is 'one of the courts of heaven, the court of a reigning seraph, a sort of a vice-queen of an angel.' Milly herself, in conversation with Lord Mark, feels suddenly her 'excluded disinherited state' in the presence of so much borrowed charm, and murmurs: 'Ah, not to go down—never, never to go down!' Lord Mark, as obtuse to her feelings as he had been when showing her the Bronzino, takes this, not as her anguished dread that she must soon sink from this exalted level, but as a reference to the fact that she no longer goes downstairs.

The continual emphasis on Milly's health faced James with a problem that he solved in his own special way. As his preface affirmed, it is 'the act of living,' not that of dying, by which characters appeal, though that appeal may be heightened 'as the conditions plot against them and prescribe the battle.' One of the leading conditions here was the degree to which Milly was threatened from the start. But the pressure of the danger does not become apparent to others beside Susan until, at the very moment of her rare pleasure before the Bronzino, the girl has a spell of faintness. In this oblique way James hints at a linkage between his themes of love and death. The very next day she goes to consult the great doctor, Sir Luke Strett, and feels, in James' equivalent for a confessional, 'as though she had been on her knees to the priest.' We never know precisely what diagnosis Sir Luke makes of her, since it is James' method to give us such knowledge only through the refracted reports of other characters. He may have felt it necessary to play down the difficult fact of physical infirmity by never saying directly what Milly's illness is, though for many readers this operates as a tedious mystification. Susan might naturally shrink away from knowing the horrible details; but when Kate says to Densher that Milly's trouble is 'not lungs, I think,' either she is lying for purposes of her own, as James' characters often do, or he is dealing in deliberate obfuscation. For as Milly behaves, she can hardly be dying of anything except tuberculosis, as Minny Temple died, at a period when no coherent cure had yet been devised.

One aspect of her situation that he penetrates with psychological depth is the relation between her delicate vitality and the will to live. Sir Luke knows that she needs love to sustain her, to relax the tension of her loneliness, and—though there is the hint in the background that he may have decided at once that there was no lasting hope for her no matter what she did—he urges her to 'take the trouble' to live.

Once again, as in *The Ambassadors*, we have a scene built upon this theme. Milly leaves the doctor's office, knowing that her situation is grave, but buoyed up by his sympathy and his challenge. She has a sense of sharing more than before in the general human lot. She starts to

walk through London's streets, a rich girl 'hoping' that she
has found the slums. She comes out finally into Regent's
Park: 'Here were wanderers anxious and tired like herself; here doubtless were hundreds of others just in the
same box. Their box, their great common anxiety, what
was it in this grim breathing-space, but the practical question of life? They could live if they would; that is, like
herself they had been told so: she saw them all about her,
on seats, digesting the information, recognizing it again as
something in a slightly different shape familiar enough,
the blessed old truth that they would live if they could.'

That reversal seems at first the easy fancy of a sheltered
ignorant girl, but James knew what he was doing. As Milly
sits meditating upon the odds against her future, upon the
rent she will have to pay, she looks around her again, with
the kind of comprehension of the favored difference in
her lot that makes the reader respond to her with full sympathy, since, no matter how favored, she too is up against
death. She saw 'her scattered melancholy comrades—some
of them so melancholy as to be down on their stomachs
in the grass, turned away, ignoring, burrowing: she saw
once more, with them, those two faces of the question between which there was so little to choose for inspiration.
It was perhaps superficially more striking that one could
live if one would; but it was more appealing, insinuating,
irresistible in short, that one would live if one could.'

Shortly after this point James introduces the image
that was to become the symbol of his title. A more or less
full account of this image, of its morphology, so to speak,
may help us to distinguish James from other symbolists. He
is so fond of animal-imagery of all sorts that it is hard to

say whether, on the occasion when he likens Aunt Maud
to an eagle with 'gilded claws,' he is preparing the way
for the contrasting image of the dove, or is simply responding to his painter's instinct to make every inch of his canvas as lively as possible. For elsewhere Aunt Maud is a
lionness, a glossy embodiment of Britannia herself; just as,
again, to Densher's eyes, Milly, worn down by the social
crush, becomes 'a Christian maiden, in the arena, mildly,
caressingly martyred,' not by the nosing 'of lions and tigers
but of domestic animals let loose as for the joke.' But there
would seem to be deliberate preparation of his chief characterizing image for Milly in her own contrasting statement that she has used 'the wisdom of the serpent' to find
in Sir Luke Strett the special man for her need. For one
quality of this 'dove' is that she is not so innocent as she
looks. She may be fooled by the new social complexity
into which she has been plunged, she may trustingly not
suspect that Aunt Maud and Kate both have designs upon
her. But in the scene where the dove-image is introduced,
she has her own strategy of how to play the part. Aunt
Maud has left the two girls together, with the request that
Milly find out for her whether Densher has returned yet
from America. One look at Kate virtually convinces Milly
that he has. Then as Kate paces the room 'like a panther,'
Milly is startled as at the foreboding of some sinister
charged energy. It is when Kate becomes aware of Milly's
strained feelings that she turns to her more gently and
pronounces her 'a dove.' This speech serves to bring out
again the contrast between the force and the delicacy of
the two. But at that moment Aunt Maud reappears, where-
upon Milly decides to appear at her 'most dovelike,' and

yet to tell her, out of loyalty to Kate's unspoken secret, that she doesn't think Densher is back.

The next use of the image is during the great climactic scene in Venice, where Milly, her dress changed for the only time in the book from mourning robes to white, makes her most radiant appearance—and her last. As Kate and Densher stand watching her across the great room, a heavy 'priceless chain' of pearls around her neck, Kate says once again, 'She's a dove.' Densher agrees that that figure best describes Milly's spirit, but he then realizes how strongly the dove-like color of pearls also enters into Kate's impression. The power of wealth, he reflects, 'was dove-like only so far as one remembered that doves have wings and wondrous flights, have them as well as tender tints and soft sounds. It even came to him dimly that such wings could . . . spread themselves for protection. Hadn't they, for that matter, lately taken an inordinate reach, and weren't Kate and Mrs. Lowder, weren't Susan Shepherd and he, wasn't *he*, in particular, nestling under them to a great increase of immediate ease?' As Kate continues to dwell on the beauty of the pearls, he realizes with a twinge that 'pearls were exactly what Merton Densher would never be able to give her.' It is at this moment that Kate, who up until now has concealed the final range of her intention, comes out with her proposal that since Milly can't live, he is to marry her for her money. Just as Kate has delivered this proposal, Milly sends across the room to them 'all the candour of her smile.'

With this ample instance of how James could extend a metaphor into a symbol, we may see him in relation to the development of modern symbolism. In several of his earliest stories, as in *The Romance of Certain Old Clothes* and *Benvolio,* he had depended on allegory in the manner of Hawthorne; and if we look closely at *Roderick Hudson,* we realize that that novel is still essentially an allegory of the life of the artist. As he went on to master all the skills of realism, he grew dissatisfied with allegory's obvious devices; and yet, particularly towards the end of his career, realistic details had become merely the covering for a content that was far from realistic. He was quite aware of the newer French movement. In fact, he stages one of the later conversations between Kate and Milly in its manner: 'Certain aspects of the connexion of these young women show for us, such is the twilight that gathers about them, in the likeness of some dim scene in a Maeterlinck play; we have positively the image, in the delicate dusk, of the figures so associated and yet so opposed, so mutually watchful: that of the angular pale princess, ostrich-plumed, black-robed, hung about with amulets, reminders, relics, mainly seated, mainly still, and that of the upright restless slow-circling lady of her court who exchanges with her, across the black water streaked with evening gleams, fitful questions and answers. The upright lady, with thick dark braids down her back, drawing over the grass a more embroidered train, makes the whole circuit, and makes it again, and the broken talk, brief and sparingly allusive, seems more to cover than to free their sense.'

Yet James was no *symboliste.* His interest in Maeterlinck was in the possibilities of a richer, more poetic drama; but he was unlike the symbolist poets in that the suggestiveness of music was not his chief concern. His own analogies for his work were always with painting or with the stage, and

he possessed none of the technical knowledge of music
that was to be exhibited by both Proust and Mann. His
leading symbols are all literary and pictorial. The four
that furnished titles for his books are biblical allusions, to
which he proceeded to give concrete embodiment with little reference to the Bible. His method of arriving at his
symbols and what he hoped to achieve by them may be
suggested by the fact that though he left an extensive
scenario for the unfinished *Ivory Tower,* this does not mention the symbol itself, any more than do his shorter notebook drafts for the other books. In other words, he did
not, like Mallarmé, start with his symbol. He reached it
only with the final development of his theme, and then
used it essentially in the older tradition of the poetic metaphor, to give concretion, as well as allusive and beautiful
extension, to his thought.

The contrast with more recent practice is striking. Unlike Mann, James was not influenced by Wagner; he has
nothing like the elaborate and studied recurrence of musical themes. And though he came to work essentially in the
genre of the fairy tale, he had not become conscious of the
possibilities of dealing explicitly with myth. That consciousness, in its modern form, was the product of a somewhat later period, of the period that had been pervaded
by Freud. James may be seen to be moving in the direction of that psychology in his suggestion through 'the sacred fount' of the springs of sexual vitality. But the full
influence of Freud was to produce the compulsive symbols
of Kafka, whose 'castle,' for instance, is not the last refinement of an already developed theme, but a dense central core of meaning beyond the reach of any articulation

that the author's mind could give to it. And, as a final de-
limitation to James' handling of symbols, there is the fact
that, again unlike subsequent writers, he had naturally
not felt the impact of more recent anthropology. He sought
for his universals in the well-lighted drawing rooms of his
time. When he groped his way back to 'the sense of the
past,' it was only to the dawn of the nineteenth century,
for the sake of a contrast with later social manners. He was
not to become aware of the obsessive presence of all times,
of the repetition of primitive patterns in civilized life, as
Eliot tried to express it through his anthropological symbol of 'the waste land.'

When James did make a thematic use of symbols, it
tended to be in the fashion of earlier poetic drama. He had
declared in his 'summing up' that the 'dramatic poem'
seemed to him 'the most beautiful thing possible,' and in
a work like *The Wings of the Dove* he was finally pro-
ducing his equivalent for it. He even made a Shakespear-
ean use of storm and calm. When Lord Mark, jealous that
Milly won't accept him, confronts her with the ugly truth
of Densher's engagement, he does it in a Venice where the
serene summer is over, where a black sky and a cold lash-
ing rain accentuate how 'all of evil' seems to have broken
out. Equally symbolically, when Sir Luke arrives for his
final visit, the storm is superseded by 'autumn sunshine,'
and the renewed beauty of the city is 'like a hanging-out
of vivid stuffs, a laying-down of fine carpets.'

But even in such renewed mellowness—to follow the book
now to its conclusion—we no longer see Milly directly.
Densher has at last become terribly aware that he has
'never been near the facts of her condition.' As he realizes

how the whole 'expensive vagueness, made up of smiles
and silences and beautiful fictions and priceless arrange-
ments,' had conspired to charm from the picture any
'shadow of pain and horror,' we probably have James'
chief reason for so muffling the question of Milly's illness.
He wanted to emphasize how her companions had fled
from reality into a 'conscious fool's paradise.' But the facts
are all there, as Densher now acutely feels them: 'the facts
of physical suffering, of incurable pain, of the chance
grimly narrowed.'

Densher is the chief means by which James keeps his romance from becoming dissevered from reality, his tale of
enchantment from becoming a tale of escape. If James created the spell of a fairy tale, he did it, as the great fabulists
have always done, for the sake of evoking universal truths.
Densher is also an important factor in preventing Susan
Stringham's intensely 'literary' version of Milly as a princess from becoming merely silly. He is in love with Kate,
and Milly, to his eyes, is no princess; she is simply 'little
Miss Theale,' the odd-looking American girl who had been
so kind to him in New York. This wholly unglamorous
view of her is also of the highest significance in the denouement, in the gradual, inescapable transformation of both
Densher and Kate.

James' moral drama here is his most thoroughgoing. The
issue between Kate and Densher is finely drawn. He is always dominated by her vitality. Even before he discerns
where her scheme is tending, he feels himself caught in
her 'wondrous silken web.' In the scene of the compact
between them, her will operates like that of a Lady Mac-
beth. When he wants to break off the pretence, Kate says:

'Do you want to kill her? We've told too many lies.' So he weakly agrees to stay in Venice for Milly, but preserves his self-respect by insisting that he will do so only on the condition that Kate will pledge her unchanged love by coming to him in his rooms for complete physical union. He clings also to the scruple that he will himself offer no proposal to Milly, but will simply wait for what she proposes. And though such a distinction may seem tenuously Jamesian, it serves to reveal the gulf that is already opening between him and Kate. For what she foresees as the result of her manipulations is, as she says, 'quite ideal'—a terrifying phrase by its utter obliviousness to any moral implications.

Densher continues to insist that he has no feelings about Milly, that he hasn't 'even the amount of curiosity that he would have had about an ordinary friend.' But as the other English people return to London and he remains behind, he begins to have increasingly a sense of 'her disconcerting poetry.' He feels her as somehow 'divine in her trust, or at any rate inscrutable in her mercy.' When, at the shock of Lord Mark's news, she has 'turned her face to the wall,' the enormity of the situation strikes home to him.

But his change is given to us only gradually and piecemeal. We learn that he has been back in London for two weeks before letting Kate know. On seeing her, he is impressed with 'how terribly well' she looks. But he finds that he can no longer feel free with her, and that oddly he must turn to her aunt in his need to talk about Milly. It is Aunt Maud who says, at the news of Milly's death, 'Our dear dove, then, as Kate calls her, has folded her wonderful wings.' But it would be unthinkable that Densher could

share with Aunt Maud the essence of what he now feels
about Milly. For, as Aunt Maud pursues her image—'unless it's more true . . . that she has spread them the wider,'
—she is thinking of the possible money. And what is uppermost for him is that when Milly had summoned him,
through Sir Luke, for their final interview, 'something had
happened to him too beautiful and too sacred to describe.
He had been, to his recovered sense, forgiven, dedicated,
blessed.'

Yet he must seek out Kate, and it is significant of the
motivating drive which James attaches to her background
that Densher finds her at her sister's, in the ugliness where
she seems so little to belong. In the last scenes between
them Kate's oppressive sense of her father's sordid evil is
always in the air, as is also Densher's sense of her enormous 'talent for life': 'What a person she would be if they
had been rich—with what a genius for the so-called great
life, what a presence for the so-called great house.' But he
has come through to the firmness of decision. They are not
to be rich. He has grown to have 'horror, almost' of her
lucidity and tenacity. As she says, in the final occurrence
of the controlling image: 'I used to call her, in my stupidity—for want of anything better—a dove. Well, she
stretched out her wings, and it was to *that* they reached.
They cover us.'

'They cover us,' Densher said.

'That's what I give you,' Kate gravely wound up. 'That's
what I've done for you.'

But even as she speaks, she knows with what liberty of
choice he will face her, that she may have either him or
the money which Milly, true to her generosity, has left

him. The wings have covered them in another sense than Kate had bargained for. Densher may insist that he 'never was in love' with Milly; but Kate replies: 'Her memory's your love. You *want* no other.'

'He heard her out in stillness, watching her face but not moving. Then he only said: "I'll marry you, mind you, in an hour."

"As we were?"

"As we were."

But she turned to the door, and her headshake was now the end. "We shall never be again as we were!" '

Kate is right. Densher has been transformed by the dead girl's hovering presence. Like the hero in any great tragedy he has arrived at the moral perception of the meaning of what has befallen him. As far as Kate is concerned, James has left the reader with the kind of choice which he believed to constitute an essential element in the relation of art to life. He has dropped one idea that was in his outline. There is no remote possibility that Kate will marry Lord Mark. But the other alternative is still in the air. This is not due to careless ambiguity. James held that an artist could convey the real complexity of life only by suggesting, through such a device of multiple choice, a wider circle beyond the restricted one he had selected to illuminate. Milly is dead. Densher has learned the meaning of loss and renunciation. Whether Kate's life has also been irrevocably altered by the brush of Milly's spirit, or whether her hard handsomeness and the desperateness of her situation will still allow her to seek her own kind of shelter beneath the spread of those opulent wings, the reader can determine only by the kind of sustained attention to the whole novel that James was always demanding. And even then James would want his reader's strongest sense to be at the end that the denseness and uncertainty of life are such that we should never pronounce too complacently or too arrogantly upon what lies ahead.

In the preface to *The Portrait of a Lady*, James discussed whether a writer could make his heroine the main support of his theme, and quoted George Eliot's conviction that 'In these frail vessels is borne onward through the ages the treasure of human affection.' But he knew that Maggie Tulliver and Rosamond Vincy, as well as Juliet and Cleopatra, were never allowed to be the 'sole ministers' of appeal. Milly Theale has almost become such. Even though the maturing of Densher may be, in its devious way, as impressive as Romeo's, he is never brought to the center of our concern. The question then presses itself whether a character like Milly's is of sufficient emotional force to carry a great work. The comparison with her original is significant. She does not possess Minny Temple's questing mind; she does not ask about the meaning of faith. The originality and the audacity which so impressed James in his cousin have been keyed down to the gentleness of the dove. But he posited for Milly the same 'excess of joy' in living, and gave to her 'crowded consciousness' the sense that it was her doom 'to live fast.' It was essential to his theme that his 'anxious fighter of the battle of life' should be arrayed against insuperable odds, that her high-strung American nerves should feel Europe too 'tough' for her.

But the issue is whether such a theme can yield more than exquisite pathos, whether it has enough substance to make tragedy. James believed that it had, that essential evil was revealed in Kate and in Lord Mark through their pursuit of the money, and that essential terror could be conveyed through Milly's own anguished horror of death. He had said in his notebook, 'She is like a creature dragged shrieking to the guillotine—to the shambles.' Densher was to make his own development of that image, as he meditated on Milly's 'unapproachable terror of the end': she 'had held with passion to her dream of a future, and she was separated from it, not shrieking indeed, but grimly, awfully silent, as one might imagine some noble young victim of the scaffold, in the French Revolution, separated at the prison-door from some object clutched for resistance.'

It is revelatory of James that, as was the case with Madame de Vionnet's loss, he again uses an image from the French Revolution, this time an image entirely aristocratic in its associations. That will mark for many readers how far James was from being capable of projecting a real American tragedy of his own time. But the controlling facts of tragedy are neither time nor place, but the urgency with which we are made to feel life and death. James has reduced his ore to the last possible refinement, but what is left is the purest metal. It is not merely the 'vague golden air' of Susan's enchantment; it is rather, as in Donne's image,

like golde to airy thinnesse beate.

There is much more of pity than of terror in Milly's confronting of fate. Her passive suffering is fitting for the deuteragonist rather than for the protagonist of a major tragedy, for a Desdemona, not for an Othello. But if James has shown again that the chords he could strike were minor, were those of renunciation, of resignation, of inner triumph in the face of outer defeat, he was not out of keeping with the spiritual history of his American epoch. Art often expresses society very obliquely, and it is notable that the most sensitive recorders of James' generation gave voice to themes akin to his. In the face of the overwhelming expansion, the local colorists felt compelled, like Sarah Orne Jewett, to commemorate the old landmarks before they should be entirely swept away and obliterated. Emily Dickinson discovered that the only way she could be a poet in such an age was by withdrawal, by depending, virtually like a Jamesian heroine, upon the richness of her own 'crowded consciousness.' And the least feminine, most robust talent of the age, Mark Twain, who may seem at the farthest pole from James, did not find his themes in the facile myths of manifest destiny or triumphant democracy. His masterpiece was also an elegy. It gave expression to the loss of the older America of his boyhood, which, no less than the milieu of Henry James and Minny Temple, had been destroyed by the onrush of the industrial revolution.

IV

'The Golden Bowl'

SOME of the consequences of the industrial revolution are oddly refracted in *The Golden Bowl*. The Ververs' wealth is of the new kind. To be sure, the product of Woollett, which Strether fastidiously refused to specify for Maria, was turned out by a New England factory that was on its way to establishing a monopoly. But the Newsomes' family fortune was only a background for James' main theme. And when money became the great tempter for Kate Croy, the source of Milly's fabulous inheritance was left entirely shrouded. Adam Verver's fortune, on the other hand, has been made entirely by himself in the post Civil War west. His again unspecified financial dealings have been as rapid as they have been vast, since he is only forty-seven, with retirement several years behind him. But he has brought his acquisitive sense into his leisure. Like so many other robber barons, he has set his heart on becoming a great collector, and gold and jewel images color, in consequence, every relationship in the novel.

Since James, not Balzac or Dreiser, is the author, most of these images have aesthetic rather than commercial connotations. They constitute the high-water mark of James' virtuosity. In the opening chapter, which presents Prince Amerigo on the eve of his marriage to Maggie Verver, the young Italian thinks of the golden bath in which he is about to be immersed as having far greater dimensions than any that had ever been supplied by the imperial loot of his remote ancestors. In Mr. Verver's view, the Prince himself is a collector's item, a costly specimen of the *cinquecento*. The book shines throughout with innumerable other such images. In two of James' most breath-takingly elaborate efforts the Prince is at one time a Palladian church, at another a dazzling pagoda. Maggie Verver becomes, to her father's eye, a lovely sculptured figure, though he is a bit vague as to whether she is a nymph or a nun. To a much greater extent than even James had previously sought for, entire scenes are centered around pictures and *objets d'art*. The culmination of this tendency is the treatment of the golden bowl.

The method of introducing and developing this symbol is the same as for the wings of the dove, though both extended and intensified. The scene in which the Prince and Charlotte Stant discover the bowl in an antique shop, while supposedly looking for a wedding present for Maggie, makes the ending of the first book. The two long chapters which lead up to and away from Mrs. Assingham's dashing the bowl to the floor form not only the climax to the fourth book, but also the most dramatic moment in the novel. It may be observed, parenthetically, that the division into books is less important here than in either *The Ambassadors* or *The Wings of the Dove*. That is not to say that James was less concerned with composition, since, as though challenged by all the works of art that he had conjured up, he bent every effort to making his structure architectural in its rigorous symmetry. The first half centers around the Prince, the second half around the

Princess. The division of each half into three books marks, in the first instance, necessary lapses of time. Between the first and second books a sufficient interval must have passed since the Prince's marriage to Maggie to make her feel that her father is too much alone and that he ought to marry again. Between the second and third books Mr. Verver's marriage with Charlotte has taken place, and Maggie has finally begun to awaken to the situation between Charlotte and the Prince. At this point the whole *donnée* is before us, as it was not in the slowly evolving two previous novels. Everything is now concentrated upon Maggie's effort to win back her husband. The pace is much swifter. There are no further lapses of time. The fourth book, which occupies over half of the second volume, takes us to the moment when Maggie confronts the Prince with her knowledge. By the end of the fifth book she has triumphed over Charlotte, and the sixth book is needed only for a brief conclusion, to dispatch Mr. Verver and Charlotte back to America.

James uses the bowl as a means of bringing to a focal point the varying and diverging complexities in such human relations. He gives no indication whether he was thinking of Blake's cryptic verses:

> Can wisdom be kept in a silver rod,
> Or love in a golden bowl?

But that latter question is insistent throughout. When the antique dealer shows the bowl to Charlotte, her first comment is: 'It may be cheap for what it is, but it will be dear, I'm afraid, for me.' We think at once of what has been too dear for her, of the fact that, despite her love for the

Prince, their marriage had been out of the question because of their lack of means. The Prince is thus the golden bowl, the 'pure and perfect crystal' which Mr. Verver has been happy to pay a big price for. But the bowl itself is quickly seen to have a flaw, and so it becomes a symbol rather for the relationship between the Prince and Charlotte—significantly he detects at once the crack beneath the gilt surface, whereas she is blind to it. Such a gift will never do for Maggie, and so they drop their pursuit, each with a refusal also to accept from the other any memento of their now dead past. They are acting here in good faith, and when he tells her that she too must marry, she answers, in the concluding lines of the first book: 'Well, I would marry, I think, to have something from you in all freedom.'

By the time of the reintroduction of the theme of the bowl, these words have taken on irony. Charlotte is married to Mr. Verver, and the old absorbing intimacy of father and daughter has thrown the other two continually by themselves. The day in the country when they finally take full advantage of their freedom is figured by the Prince as 'a great gold cup that we must somehow drain together.' A similar sounding of the theme is made by Maggie when, waking to the loss of her husband, she speaks of 'the full cup' of her need of him. But the most brilliant demonstration in all James' work of what he could do with a symbol is in those two climactic scenes, between Maggie and Fanny Assingham, and then between Maggie and the Prince. Maggie herself has now stumbled upon the bowl while looking for a remembrance for her father's birthday; and from certain details that the dealer

unwittingly let fall, she has pieced together the earlier
scene in his shop, and has seen the bowl as the sign of her
husband's intimacy with Charlotte. She has placed it in
the center of her mantel to confront him as soon as he
comes in, but now that she feels her whole future to be
weighted by the bowl, she has a foreboding that perhaps
the Prince may never again enter her room. Mrs. Assingham, who has known about the others' relation, but has
been determined to keep it from Maggie, tells her that her
whole idea 'has a crack,' just as the bowl has. Insisting
that nothing stands between Maggie and the Prince, she
dramatically smashes the bowl on the polished floor. How
thoroughly James' imagination was imbued with the
devices of the fairy story is attested by the fact that the
Prince instantly appears, just as though he was a genie
released by the breaking of an evil spell. Though that comparison is not made, such is the effect.

As Maggie gathers up the three pieces into which the
bowl has split, the two halves of the cup itself and 'the
solid detached foot,' the urgent question for her is what
can be salvaged from the triangle in which she is involved. The bowl is now the token of her knowledge, of
the fact that she hasn't been such an innocent fool as the
Prince may have supposed. As she confronts him with this,
the dawning possibility of his new need of her seems to
flicker over the fragments. The dramatic 'thickness' of
such scenes can obviously not be paraphrased, since their
excitement depends on the ranging play of association that
is in the air at every moment. The Prince and Maggie are
talking about the actual bowl, but other meanings are more
shiftingly alive:

' "And what, pray, *was* the price?"

She paused again a little. "It was high certainly—for those fragments. I think I feel as I look at them there rather ashamed to say."

The Prince then again looked at them; he might have been growing used to the sight. "But shall you at least get your money back?" '

That remains the crucial question for the rest of the novel, whether the Ververs have paid too much for their Prince. As Maggie says to Mrs. Assingham, she wants 'the golden bowl—as it *was* to have been . . . The bowl with all our happiness in it. The bowl without the crack.' By the end that is what she has gained. In the closing scene James again finds his own kind of use for a work of art. Maggie and her father are commenting on the fineness of 'the early Florentine sacred subject' that he had given her on her marriage; but as they look at the picture, they are really exchanging views on the resolution of the situation. When Mr. Verver says, '*Le compte y est*. You've got some good things,' the Prince falls under his glance as the best attestation 'of a rare power of purchase.' And when Maggie and her husband are left alone at last, the mingled images of beauty and wealth are still sustained. She reflects that here is 'the golden fruit that had shone from afar.' But the gold is more substantial than that. She knows now that she is going 'to be paid in full.' As the Prince turns to her for their final embrace, he 'might have been holding out the money bag for her to come and take it.'

The expertness with which James has brought out so many connotations latent in the bowl has kept that symbol from ever becoming frozen or schematized. He has thus un-

questionably succeeded in making an *objet d'art* the co-
hesive center of his own intricate creation. But other questions are raised by those curiously mixed final images.
When there is so much gold that it pervades even the vocabulary of love, is that a sign of life or of death? What
sort of world is being portrayed, and how are we to
judge it?

In the view of Colonel Assingham, the most detached
observer here, life is largely 'a matter of pecuniary arrangement,' and Maggie Verver is 'more than anything else the
young woman who has a million a year.' But the American
world into which he is launched is far less simple for the
Prince. He figures it, through his early memory of Poe's
Narrative of A. Gordon Pym, as 'a dazzling curtain of light,
concealing as darkness conceals, yet of the colour of milk
or of snow.' He has been used to curtains of black and
doesn't know what to expect in Maggie's realm of moral
innocence, where the very existence of evil seems to be lost
in the shrouding 'white mist.' [1] That Americans are 'incredibly romantic,' he avows to her at the start. 'Of course
we are,' she answers. 'That's just what makes everything
so nice for us.'

James has clearly bent his attention to showing how
nice that can be. He has continued down the vistas that
opened for him in *The Wings of the Dove.* The Ververs
are far richer even than Milly Theale; and if she was a
pretended princess, Maggie Verver's marriage has made
her an actual one. More than that, her father is virtually

[1] I have already discussed some further implications of this image of
whiteness in comparing James' kind of symbolism with the allegory
and symbolism of Hawthorne and Melville, in *American Renaissance,*
pp. 301-5.

a king: he is likened to Alexander 'furnished with the spoils of Darius.' The character most comparable to Adam Verver in James' earlier work is Christopher Newman, in *The American,* and that comparison is instructive for James' development. The first names of both men call attention to the quality that James was most concerned to endow them with: both are discoverers of new worlds, just as, in turn, Prince Amerigo's name symbolizes how he must be a re-discoverer of America, or of what may prove even harder, of Americans. What Newman and Mr. Verver also have in common is their newness: it would hardly seem accidental that both syllables of the latter's surname suggest spring. Both too have had their moments of vision in which the mere amassing of money came to seem futile. An amusing corroboration of the exorbitant demands raised by James' later imagination is that the financial deal which brought home that truth to Newman was originally for sixty thousand dollars, but was changed in the revision to half a million. But whereas Newman came to Europe with a quiet eagerness for wider experience, Mr. Verver brought along his far vaster fortune and a scheme. His 'business of the future' was 'to rifle the Golden Isles.' He might, like James himself, have been a friend of Mrs. Jack Gardner's, so typical was his desire of our era of 'the pillage of the past,' as Lewis Mumford has called it. Mr. Verver's vision, his 'peak in Darien,' as James calls it, has stretched out before him the gleaming possibility of giving to his home town, American City, situated somewhat dimly beyond the Mississippi, a whole museum complete with contents. He has reached even as far as Henry Ford was going to: he would like even to transport 'the little old church' from his English estate 'for its simple sweetness.' Never, indeed, have the claims of the collector been pitched higher: he conceives his dedicated rôle 'as equal somehow' to that of 'the great seers, the invokers and encouragers of beauty—and he didn't after all perhaps dangle so far below the great producers and creators.'

The odd thing is that James seems to take Mr. Verver at his own estimate. Furthermore, though he posits for him an 'acquisitive power' that amounted to 'a special genius,' James deliberately invests him also with a paradisal innocence. He is simplicity incarnate. In contrast with the flamboyant architectural images for the Prince, his face suggests 'a small decent room, clean-swept.' Seated at the head of his table, he is 'like a little boy shyly entertaining in virtue of some imposed rank . . . quite as an infant king is the representative of a dynasty.' He seems at times even more youthful than the Principino, his grandson, and his daughter treats him much as she used to treat her doll.

In drawing such a character James is at the farthest remove from Balzac, whose most brilliant moral studies are those of the transforming and corrupting power which wealth exercises upon its possessor. James was always ready to confess that he did not have the shadowiest notion of business; but by picking a character like Adam Verver he obligated himself to some knowledge of the type of men who were making the great American fortunes—if not Dreiser's knowledge in *The Financier* and *The Titan,* at least that which Edith Wharton could show in *The Custom of the Country.* Without such knowledge he laid himself wide open to the most serious charge that can be levelled against a great novelist, what Yvor Winters has instanced, in the case of *The Spoils of Poynton,* as the split between manners and morals, the lack of congruity between the environment which would have produced a character and the traits which the author has imputed to him. Mr. Verver's moral tone is far more like that of a benevolent Swedenborgian than it is like that of either John D. Rockefeller or Jay Gould.

If James failed to see how vulnerable he was in his portrait of Mr. Verver, it may have been because his attention was concentrated on something else. It was the rule of his later air-tight structures, a rule under which even Edith Wharton finally grew restive, that every detail was to be subordinated to his main theme. And here that theme was again composed around his heroine. Through her, as through Milly Theale, he wanted to give his last quintessential expression to a quality which had long haunted him, not the intense yearning for life, but another phase of the American character as he had known it, its baffled and baffling innocence in contrast with the experience of Europeans. That again is a minor-keyed and feminine quality, more convincing in a daughter than in a father. But when Mrs. Assingham goes to the length of saying that Maggie 'wasn't born to know evil, she must never know it,' we are back in the world of Hawthorne, of Hilda and her doves in *The Marble Faun.* The flinching from experience on the part of Hawthorne's blonde girls was what D. H. Lawrence found the most repellent of American traits; and it must be added that James intended Maggie's 'goodness' which Colonel Assingham finds 'awfully quaint,' to have its own initiation into evil.

But quaint or not, James believed in the moral fineness

and sweetness of the old-time simpler America, and believed, too, that even if Mr. Verver was a billionaire, he
could still be colored by those qualities. From the point
of view of Charlotte's sophistication, the continued intimacy between Maggie and her father is an astonishing
'make-believe': 'They were fairly at times, the dear things,
like children playing at paying visits, playing at "Mr.
Thompson and Mrs. Fane," each hoping that the other
would really stay to tea.' But the core of James' intention
in this relationship remains what it had been when he was
first thinking of making a short story on the theme and
had declared in his notebook: 'The *subject* is really the
pathetic simplicity and good faith of the father and daughter in their abandonment.'

Such a relationship raises some interesting questions
about James' grasp of psychology. He had altered several
details which had fitted his original plan for a short piece,
especially the simultaneity of the double marriage, and the
precipitation of the situation by the daughter's French
husband finding himself more attracted by his father-in-
law's young wife. James made the Prince's adultery less
reprehensible by having him break with his past in all
honesty, only to find it catch up with him unexpectedly
through Maggie's eagerness to have her father marry
Charlotte. But James held to the important contributing
factor, the reason why the lovers were thrown together so
often, as he had first outlined it: 'A necessary basis . . .
must have been an intense and exceptional degree of attachment between the father and daughter—he peculiarly
paternal, she passionately filial.'

James wrote with a knowledge of the sophisticated so-

ciety of his day. He had led up to his notebook entry with
some general reflections on the international marriage, and
how its 'queer crudity' offered 'plenty of opportunity for
satiric fiction.' Observing, too, in the era that had united
Lord Randolph Churchill with Jennie Jerome of Roches-
ter, N. Y., that it was always the European man who married the American girl, 'never the other way round,' he
then went on to contrast the American girl with the American man. He had been impressed with what E. L. Godkin
had said to him about the growing cleavage between the
two: the one 'with her comparative leisure, culture, grace,
social instincts, artistic ambitions'; the other 'immersed in
the ferocity of business with no time for any but the most
sordid interests, purely commercial, professional, democratic and political.' One questions whether Godkin had
used the word 'democratic' in just that sequence, though
Henry Adams might have. James' conclusion about the
relation of the sexes was also like that of Adams: 'This divorce is rapidly becoming a gulf—an abyss of inequality,
the like of which has never before been seen under the
sun.'

But James did not satirize the international marriage in
The Golden Bowl. No more did he develop that cleavage
between the sexes. Instead he distributed what he had
noted as the feminine traits between Maggie and her father. Another limitation that would be even more puzzling
to the modern psychologist is the view James took of their
relationship. Though Charlotte may protest that her husband treats her 'as of less importance to him than some
other woman,' James regards this intimacy between father
and daughter as 'perfectly natural,' exceptionally close, to

be sure, and naively innocent, but without a trace of the pathological fixation that our novelists would now see in it. James occupies a curious border line between the older psychologists like Hawthorne or George Eliot, whose concerns were primarily religious and ethical, and the post-Freudians. When, in *The Bostonians,* he wanted to make a study of Olive Chancellor's violent possessiveness over Verena Tarrant, he could do it out of his knowledge 'of those friendships between women which are so common in New England.' But though he could understand Lesbianism without having to give it a name, just as he could understand the corruption of the children in *The Turn of the Screw,* he was elsewhere oblivious to sexual distortions which would seem an almost inevitable concomitant of the situations he posits. Take, for instance, *The Pupil,* where, in contrast with Mann's *Death in Venice,* there is no basis in homosexual attraction, and a consequent vagueness, as the story is handled, in accounting for why the tutor's attachment to his charge is so strong as to make him destroy his prospects on the boy's account. What it comes down to, again and again, is that James' characters tend to live, as has often been objected, merely off the tops of their minds. This is what caused a representative modern psychologist like Gide to conclude that James, 'in himself, is not interesting; he is only intelligent.' And what bothers Gide most in James' characters is the excessive functioning of their analytical powers, whereas 'all the weight of the flesh is absent, and all the shaggy, tangled undergrowth, all the wild darkness . . .' But in works as different as *The Turn of the Screw* and *The Wings of the Dove,* James showed an extraordinary command of his own kind of darkness, not the darkness of passion, but the darkness of moral evil.

As far as *The Golden Bowl* is concerned, James was again bent on conjuring up a world of magical enchantment. If we want to understand his aims, we had better follow the first rule of criticism and turn to what he has done rather than to what he hasn't. Instead of belaboring further his social and psychological limitations, it is more revelatory to examine the positive values which he found in such a world. As usual we arrive at those values through a series of diverse registers. To a casual glance Fanny Assingham may seem the typical spokesman for James' milieu. It is she who enunciates the proposition upon which his narratives seem most to depend, that 'the forms . . . are two-thirds of conduct.' It is she who asks, 'What is morality but high intelligence?' It is she who seems most supplied with supercharged Jamesian adjectives. It is she, indeed, who pronounces Charlotte no less than 'sublime' for coming back from America to see her old school friend through her marriage with the Prince—though it remains for Charlotte and the Prince themselves to reach the ultimate transvaluation of ordinary meanings when they pronounce as nothing less than 'sacred' their obligation to conceal their adultery from the trusting Ververs.

Fanny is the champion player of that favorite Jamesian game of scrutinizing the motives of her friends. She has all the leisure necessary to develop her skill. Indeed, she says, at the time of the Prince's marriage, that she will give her life 'for the next year or two, if necessary' to finding a husband for Charlotte. Many readers have objected to her relentless overinterpretation of the least detail as being typical of what is worst in James. But a point generally overlooked is that James has provided her with a husband who is himself the staunchest anti-Jacobite on record. In the first of their interminable conversations, Fanny starts wondering why Charlotte has come back, only to have the Colonel answer, 'What's the good of asking yourself if you know you don't know?' That sets the tone for all his rejoinders. When Fanny goes on worrying, 'How will it do, how will it do?' he puffs his cigar: 'It will do, I daresay, without your wringing your hands over it.' He also undercuts her adjectives. At her description of 'astonishing little Maggie,' ' "Is Maggie then astonishing too?" . . . he gloomed out of the window.' And when Fanny, undeterred, still pursues her flight and declares that she is beginning to make Maggie out as even 'rather extraordinary,' ' "You certainly will if you can," the Colonel resignedly remarked.'

The cynical Colonel is certainly not the author's spokesman, but he is a valuable facet of humor amid the too frequent solemnities of James' later style. What, however, should be just as clear is that Fanny's words are not to be treated as gospel either. She is perfectly willing to lie, and her sharp but barren lucidity is sufficient token that in James' scale of values there is a higher morality than that of 'high intelligence.'

What that morality consists in, James means to express through the final basis on which Maggie and the Prince are re-united. He views Amerigo sympathetically throughout. He makes him insist to Fanny on his 'good faith'; and almost his first words to Maggie are an assurance that he doesn't 'lie nor dissemble nor deceive.' In trying to com-

prehend his father-in-law, the Prince hits upon a formula
that he might almost have found in *The Theory of the
Leisure Class*. He figures that he is 'allying himself to science, for what was science but the absence of prejudice
backed by the presence of money?' The life that the
Ververs expect him to lead would also corroborate Veblen,
whose book James had probably not read, though Howells
had recognized its great importance in a review. The Prince
is the extreme case of the man who is expected to be rather
than to do, a shining exhibit of conspicuous waste. Colonel
Assingham is right in asserting that the reason why
Amerigo is tempted into his affair with Charlotte is that he
has nothing whatever to occupy him. But the emptiness of
his existence is even greater than James was aware. In concentrating so excessively on the personal relations of his
quadrangle, he imagined for the Prince no further rôle
than that of arranging his rare books and balloting once at
his club. His height of 'sacrifice' is giving up on one occasion the opportunity of dressing for dinner.

Despite the evidence of such details, James was not sati-
rizing either the Prince or the Ververs. For he was capable
of finding enough positive content in his heroine's drama
to absorb him wholly, and to let him assert, just as he was
finishing the book, that it was the best he had 'ever done.'
Its dynamics are provided entirely by Maggie, who com-
bines Milly Theale's capacity for devotion with Kate Croy's
strength of will. James' values of the heart, in contrast to
those of the mere intelligence, are realized in her to the
full. She thus provides us with material for understanding
his conception both of love and of religion. How much she
embraces under the former, James attests in the passage

where he has her declare to Fanny: ' "I can bear anything . . . For love."

Fanny hesitated. "Of your father?"

"For love," Maggie repeated.

It kept her friend watching. "Of your husband?"

"For love," Maggie said again.'

James means to convey thus the rare inclusiveness of her
generosity; but the reader's mind is likely to be crossed
also by a less pleasant aspect, by something slightly sickening in this wide-open declaration of being in love with
love, without discrimination between kinds.

Yet Maggie is clear enough about what she wants when
she sets out to win back her husband. The great scene,
which James intensifies by framing in a way comparable to
Strether's recognition on the river, is that in the fifth
book, wherein Maggie perceives all the implications of
what she is trying to salvage. The frame is provided by
a great lighted window of the card-room in which the
others are playing bridge, while Maggie paces up and
down the terrace, looking in at them. Such a projection
enables James to condense in a single visual image all the
essential aspects of his drama: 'The facts of the situation
were upright for her round the green cloth and the silver
flambeaux; the fact of her father's wife's lover facing his
mistress; the fact of her father sitting all unsounded and
unblinking, between them; the fact of Charlotte keeping
it up, keeping up everything, across the table, with her
husband beside her; the fact of Fanny Assingham, wonderful creature, placed opposite to the three and knowing
more about each, probably, when one came to think, than
either of them knew of either.'

This is the perfect image for the Jamesian game. And the key to his kind of inner drama lies in Maggie's consciousness that though merely an absent observer, she is 'presumably more present to the attention of each than the next card to be played.' Breathless suspense is created by her sudden awareness that she might smash this harmony like the stroke of doom. The images here are extremely violent. Her temptation to cry out in denunciation assaults her, 'as a beast might have leaped at her throat.' She knows horror for the first time, 'the horror of finding evil seated all at its ease, where she had only dreamed of good; the horror of the thing hideously *behind,* behind so much trusted, so much pretended, nobleness, cleverness, tenderness.' But as she moves through the storm-charged night to the end of the terrace and around the house, she faces her alternatives with re-conquered control. The lighted empty drawing-room strikes her 'like a stage again awaiting a drama . . . a scene she might people, by the press of her spring, either with serenities and dignities and decencies, or with terrors and shambles and ruins, things as ugly as those formless fragments of her golden bowl she was trying so hard to pick up.'

The violence is never externalized. If Maggie is finally to have the golden bowl 'as it was to have been,' the decorum of appearances must be kept. She must defeat Charlotte without disturbing the peace, especially that of her father. But the scenes between Maggie and Charlotte are as charged with the energy of the unspoken as any that James ever wrote. As Maggie watches Charlotte leave the card-table, she has the sensation that a caged beast has escaped and is coming after her. But in the final conflict be-

tween them, the aggressiveness is all Maggie's. James makes
her American self-reliance the equivalent of a religion. She
is explicitly a Catholic, as her mother had been, but in her
time of crisis, in contrast with Hawthorne's Hilda, she finds
that she has no need of the Church. James' brief picture
of Father Mitchell, 'good hungry holy man,' prattling and
twiddling his thumbs over his satisfied stomach, is devastating, but he seems not to have intended any general satire
of Catholicism, for which he elsewhere expressed respect
as a conserving institution. His point is not that the Church
has failed Maggie, but that her love and her own will are
enough.

In contrast with Strether and Milly, and, indeed, with
Newman, with Daisy Miller, with Isabel Archer, and with
most of James' other Americans in Europe, the Ververs are
not faced with defeat or renunciation, but with the consequences of complete triumph. The difference in James'
ability to portray such values is considerable. He was aware
of the danger of making Maggie overweening in her victory; and so she allows Charlotte to preserve her pride by
having the last word, and by making it appear as though
she herself had chosen to take Mr. Verver back to America.
In addition, Maggie feels the pathos in Charlotte's situation. In one extraordinary passage when Charlotte is showing some visitors the art-treasures of the house, she becomes
a tortured lecturer on herself as she recites her lesson: 'The
largest of the three pieces has the rare peculiarity that the
garlands looped round it, which as you see are the finest
possible *vieux Saxe,* aren't of the same origin or period, or
even, wonderful as they are, of a taste quite so perfect.'
Unlike the Ververs, Charlotte, who has been brought up

in Europe, is 'of a corrupt generation.' Yet as Maggie hears her go on, '. . . its value as a specimen is I believe almost inestimable,' she is surprised that her own eyes are filled with tears. The quaver in Charlotte's voice is 'like the shriek of a soul in pain,' and the unspoken question with which Maggie looks across the room to her father is, 'Can't she be stopped? Hasn't she done it *enough?*'

Exactly what Mr. Verver thinks and feels about the situation is never given to us directly, since no word about it is allowed to pass between daughter and father. But James is clearly proud of Mr. Verver's share in the success. He notes once that this collector applies 'the same measure of value to such different pieces of property as old Persian carpets . . . and new human acquisitions,' but he never probes the implications of that anomaly. In a less special world, such a warping of fundamental values would have caused Mr. Verver to be portrayed as a Midas whose touch finally turned gold to horror. But Mr. Verver is happy to win back his rightful possession of his wife, and to take her along with his other museum-pieces as a benefaction to American City. His participation in the final action is symbolized by one of James' most strangely ambiguous images. The 'little meditative man' is described as 'weaving his own spell,' and presently that magic takes the form of an invisible silken halter or lasso around Charlotte's neck, to every twitch of which she must respond. This image is repeated on three occasions, and what James seems to want to keep uppermost through it is the unobtrusive smoothness of his 'dear man's' dealings. But James' neglect of the cruelty in such a cord, silken though it be, is nothing short of obscene.

James' failure to examine the premises of Mr. Verver's power led Ferner Nuhn to the ingenious conjecture of what this novel would have been like if recorded from Charlotte's point of view. He concluded that even 'the lovely Princess of the fairy tale' might then have turned out instead 'to be the bad witch.' James' treatment of Maggie, however, unlike his treatment of her father, is not incoherent. She has had her initiation into evil. She has won not only the Prince's respect for her forebearance, but also his deep love. As a result of what she has passed through, she can meet him now on the level of his mature wisdom: 'Everything's terrible, cara—in the heart of man.' And yet, through the very balanced manipulation of his denouement, James has shown the limitation with which Mark Ambient, one of his author-narrators, charged himself. He has 'arranged things too much . . . smoothed them down and rounded them off and tucked them in— done everything to them that life doesn't do.' In consequence, we can hardly escape feeling that Maggie, once more like Hilda, both has her cake and eats it too. She seems to get an unnatural knowledge of evil since she keeps her innocence intact.

Or perhaps the unsatisfactory nature of the positive values in this novel may be better described through the contrast between victory and defeat. In both *The Ambassadors* and *The Wings of the Dove* we are moved most deeply by loss and suffering. But there is an intrusion of complacence when Maggie, imaged repeatedly as a dancing girl, is said to be having 'the time of her life' in her sustained act. One reason why James was less convincing in imagining success was that he was unable to conceive it in any heroic form. In this he was a sensitive register of a time when American success was so crassly materialistic that, as we have noted, nearly all the enduring writers from that time voiced their opposition. But here, in his detachment, James was trying to invest his triumphant Americans with qualities they could hardly possess.

Or we may put it technically, that he did not find the 'objective correlative' for his theme. In every case we have seen that James' values went deep into his own past, even when he translated them into so different a milieu as Milly Theale's was from Minny Temple's. But when such innocent affection, such close paternal and filial relationships as characterized the James' family, are projected into a realm so unlike the one into which James had been born, we have reached the breaking point of credibility. Love is not enough to redeem a world like Maggie Verver's, as we can tell by a single glance ahead at the inevitably futile existence that any such Prince and Princess must continue to lead. A contrast with *The Scarlet Letter* recalls that the adultery there brought out a festering growth of hypocrisy and pride and vengefulness through which Hester Prynne had to struggle alone towards her redemption. And even if Hawthorne's narrative, like James', concentrated upon the personal relations of a very few characters, Hawthorne gave, through the depth of his moral perception, a sense of the larger society of which his characters were part. The inadequacy of *The Golden Bowl* in this respect makes it finally a decadent book, in the strict sense in which decadence was defined by Orage, as 'the substitution of the part for the whole.'

James himself suggested the weakness of this book when

putting his finger on that of *The American.* In pointing out the lack of verisimilitude in having the Bellegardes relinquish the chance of getting Newman's money, he was led into a definition of romance which not only takes the discussion of Hawthorne's prefaces a step further, but also constitutes one of the major formulations about the nature of the nineteenth-century novel. James knew, from his own immersion in the development of that novel, that the separation, in the name of a self-conscious realism, between reality and romance, is false. He insists that 'the men of largest responding imagination before the human scene,' such as Balzac, commit themselves to both modes; that 'it would be impossible to have a more romantic temper than Flaubert's Madame Bovary, and yet nothing less resembles a romance than the record of her adventures.' But James does not blur the distinction: 'The real represents to my perception the things we cannot possibly *not* know, sooner or later, in one way or another . . . The romantic stands, on the other hand, for the things that, with all the facilities in the world, all the wealth and all the courage and all the wit and all the adventure, we never *can* directly know; the things that can reach us only through the beautiful circuit and subterfuge of our thought and our desire.'

We can tell from such a passage that, despite the conventional classification, James was very little of a realist. He held the test for the romance to be that whereas it deals with 'experience liberated,' with 'experience disengaged, disembroiled, disencumbered, exempt from the conditions that we usually know to attach to it,' it must not fail too patently to make its events correspond to our sense 'of the way things happen.' (Hawthorne, using the vocabulary of the mid-century, had said that the writer of romance may 'so manage his atmospherical medium' as to mellow the lights or enrich the shadows of his picture, but that he must not 'swerve aside from the truth of the human heart.') When James looked back to *The American,* after an interval of over thirty years, he believed that he had so failed. He was not to have our chance of seeing *The Golden Bowl* at that distance. But, whereas it now appears that *The Wings of the Dove* is his superlative example—perhaps the superlative example in our literature—of what can be liberated 'through the beautiful circuit and subterfuge' of thought and desire, *The Golden Bowl* forces upon our attention too many flagrant lapses in the way things happen both in the personal and in the wider social sphere. With all its magnificence, it is almost as hollow of real life as the châteaux that had risen along Fifth Avenue and that had also crowded out the old Newport world that James remembered.

V

'The American Scene' and 'The Ivory Tower'

JAMES needed to break the web of his own enchantment. He grew aware, even in the midst of his most abundant production, of the necessity for fresh observation. His three miraculous years had included, beyond the three novels, his two-volume memorial biography of Story, the American sculptor of Hawthorne's period in Rome, and seven or eight short tales. But even before he had finished *The Golden Bowl,* he was writing to Howells: 'I am hungry for Material, whatever I may be moved to do with it.' The source for new material, he felt, could only be America, which, with his absence of over twenty years, had come to be almost as romantic—as other—as Europe had been for his early dreams. The America he wanted most to see was not that of his old memories, but the sweep of the country from New York to Florida and out to California. William wrote serio-comic warnings against the scheme: how, for instance, would Henry's nerves react to the abomination of seeing his fellow countrymen eat their boiled eggs broken into a cup with butter, to say nothing of hearing their 'ignobly awful' vocalization? But when Henry responded that shocks of all kinds were what he longed for, William rejoiced in the prospect of his brother's 'rejuvenation.'

On the eve of his return, Herbert Croly summed up the whole question of James' expatriation as sensibly as it has ever been put. Notwithstanding his concern with the promise of American life, Croly knew that such life was still 'in the making.' Almost echoing Tocqueville, he said that America's 'social forms are confused and indefinite; its social types either local or evasive or impermanent.' He believed this comment to be relevant to James' case, since 'in such a society the permanent aspects which a novelist may fix, tend to be, as the work of Mr. Howells shows, somewhat unimportant.' That quiet formulation seems very just. Our critics of the thirties, in their enthusiasm over the fact that Howells was moving towards the values of socialism, have tended to overlook that what he himself created was pretty mild. He was a sensitive and honest recorder of manners and customs, but no novel of his quite possesses the kind of sustained wholeness that stirs a reader's imagination.

James had perceived, as early as 1871, that 'the face of nature and civilization' in America would 'yield its secrets only to a really grasping imagination,' and had added: 'This I think Howells lacks.' But not to beg the question of what James lacked or what he evaded, let Croly finish his formulation: 'To possess much of the style and intellectual vision which one's countrymen need, and yet to be so divided from them that you cannot help them in their poverty, seems to me a high price to pay for the advantages of Mr. James' expatriation. Yet I am not bold enough to say that the price is too high. An achievement so extraordinary and so individual as that of Henry James is absolutely its own justification, and American critics should recognize this plain condition by considering it chiefly upon its own merits, rather than upon its defects or effects.'

In exposing himself more broadly to the American scene than ever before, James said that he was 'hag-ridden by the twin demons of observation and imagination.' The resulting book of impressions is one of the curiosities of our literature. It reads as though James had explicitly decided to be Emerson's 'transparent eyeball' and nothing else, as though the rules of the game prohibited him from going beyond what he had seen for himself. The effect is as if a camera was clicking nervously over every surface it encountered; and we have to piece together for ourselves the meaning of scenes both in and out of historical focus.

From his first glimpse from shipboard of the villas along the New Jersey shore as a string 'of more or less monstrous pearls,' he was struck everywhere by the immodest lack of form. His search for sustaining defenses against the senseless onrush of chaos reveals the social basis of his taste. The new iron fence around the Harvard Yard appealed to him as a satisfactory symbol for the protection of 'the place to think' from the encroachments of the world outside, a world which he figured as 'a huge Rappacini-garden, rank with each variety of the poison-plant of the money passion.'

American speech appalled him quite as much as his brother had anticipated. He found the utterance of the younger generation 'destitute of any approach to an emission of the consonant,' and thereby reduced to 'a mere helpless slobber of disconnected vowel noises,' presumably characterizing thus the great American 'uh.' He believed our lack of settled manners to be a root cause for our lack of vocal tone. He listened to conversation everywhere, and in New York's East-side cafés he felt that he had entered 'the torture-rooms of the living idiom,' that he was hearing the first

rasping shrieks of 'the Accent of the Future.' He had much
more to say on the question of our speech, in an address
to the graduating class at Bryn Mawr, wherein he granted
that language must always be 'a living organism, fed by
the very breath of those who employ it,' and yet countered
with his conviction that for good taste 'the conservative
influence' must always predominate.

Judgment of language is inevitably a judgment of society, and the elaborations of James' latest manner are involved with what he wanted and what he did not find in
American life. William believed that *The American Scene*
was in its own peculiar way 'supremely great,' that Henry's
perceptions did produce the illusion of solid objects, even
though they seemed to be made '(like the "ghost" at the
Polytechnic) wholly out of impalpable materials, air, and
the prismatic interferences of light, ingeniously focused by
mirrors upon empty space.' Yet he could not help ejacu-
lating: 'For gleams and innuendoes and felicitous verbal
insinuations you are unapproachable, but the *core* of literature is solid. Give it to us *once* again!' Henry remained
blandly confident that his latest manner was the supplest
for what he had to say, but William's instinct was closer
to the road our subsequent writers have taken. William
felt that what his own generation needed was 'the sudden
word, the unmediated transition,' and loved Mr. Dooley
for providing them. Edith Wharton knew how greatly
Henry had also enjoyed Mr. Dooley's comments on the
world, and brought them together in New York. Her description of their encounter dramatizes the polar issue between them: 'I perceived, as I watched them after dinner,
that Peter Dunne was floundering helplessly in the heavy

seas of James' parentheses; and the next time we met, after speaking of his delight in having at last seen James, he added mournfully: "What a pity it takes him so long to say anything! Everything he said was so splendid—but I felt like telling him all the time—'Just spit it right up into Popper's hand.' " '

Many readers have pronounced a similar judgment on the style of *The American Scene,* where both the choice and the arrangement of words correspond to the ultimate elaboration of James' own mental processes, but hardly at all to anyone else's spoken idiom. This was where he had arrived through cultivating the art of dictation ever since the eighteen nineties.[1] Our recent prose, as inaugurated by Sherwood Anderson and Lardner and Hemingway, has found its sources of life in James' 'torture-rooms'; and poets as distant from one another as Frost and Cummings have demonstrated their return to Emerson's prime belief that the language of poetry takes its impulse from the speech of the common man. James looked at the common man with shy friendliness, but believed that democracy inevitably levels down. Whenever he started generalizing about the America of 1905 and trusted his impressions alone to lead him to social truths, he was apt to end up with odd propositions. When he went to Salem and asked his way to the House of the Seven Gables, he was astounded to find that he had directed his question to an Italian who knew no English. He worried a good deal about what the

---

[1] In a note made in 1914 James indicated just when he started this practice: 'In (& for) July 1896 went down to Bournemouth to escape the uproar in town. Had engaged W. McAlpin as amanuensis that winter-spring and begun the practice of dictating. Went on with it over *In the Cage* and *What Maisie Knew.*'

new aliens from southern and central Europe would do to our Anglo-Saxon culture, and drifted dangerously close to a doctrine of racism. But he could be even more misled when seizing upon something to praise, for positives to balance his negatives. The then emergent institution of the Country Club, being so unlike European exclusiveness, impressed him as 'one of the great garden-lamps in which the flame of Democracy burns whitest and steadiest.' Such a notion was hardly to be verified by Sinclair Lewis, or by those deeply moving passages in *An American Tragedy* where the country club becomes a symbol of all the brittle glamour from which Clyde Griffiths feels himself excluded.

Yet James saw the object as it really was whenever his disciplined eye alone could serve him, and in particular, therefore, whenever he was confronted with American works of art. Despite his admiration for Saint-Gaudens' Sherman, he confessed his uneasiness at the Destroyer's horse being led by 'a beautiful American girl.' His taste thus landed him at the center of a sound social judgment: he was suspicious 'of all attempts, however glittering and golden, to confound destroyers with benefactors.' He also saw things in New York architecture that only our Chicago pioneers of the modern movement were then aware of. He reflected that 'nowhere else does pecuniary power so beat its wings in the void' as in New York; and he read 'the whole costly up-town demonstration' of its imitative châteaux 'as a record, in the last analysis, of individual loneliness.' Although an inheritor of the age of the individual, the conflicting crudities of the unplanned blocks of Riverside Heights spoke to him as 'the vividest of lectures on the subject of individualism.' In a passage where

his eye carried him much farther than his amorphous social philosophy could have followed, he was led to ask:
'Why should conformity and subordination, that acceptance of control and assent to collectivism in the name of
which our age has seen such dreary things done, become
on a given occasion the one *not* vulgar way of meeting a
problem?'

He took back to his retreat at Rye an overwhelming
sensation of America's new 'material and political power' as
being 'almost cruelly charmless.' He knew now, as he had
not known when conjuring up Mr. Verver's American City,
how the recklessly impermanent sky-scrapers had risen 'by
the breath of an interested passion . . . restless beyond
all passions.' He had felt that passion so dominating
throughout the land that he had wryly concluded that
'the main American formula' was 'Make so much money
that you won't mind anything.' He had concluded also
that if you didn't accept that formula, 'America is no
place for you.' He sensed finally that for the millions who
had no Lamb House, Rye, to escape to, and who had to
continue to live under the encroaching shadow of the new
Trusts, there might be only the 'freedom to grow up to be
blighted.'

How such knowledge served to add a new energy and
conviction to his stories may be illustrated by following
through his notebooks the evolution of two of them, *The
Special Type,* issued in the year before his trip to America,
and *A Round of Visits,* which, appearing in 1910, was the
last short story that he published. Both deal with situations
which demanded for their sense of reality a knowledge of
how wealth exercises its power. What was most lacking in

The Golden Bowl were the strong passions and the violent personalities of the age of Commodore Vanderbilt; and yet *The Special Type* took its inception from what James had been told about the divorce of one of the Vanderbilt sons: that he had engaged a demi-mondaine 'in Paris to *s'afficher* with him in order to force his virago of a wife to divorce him.' James made that note in 1895, and, as was his frequent practice, he allowed the idea to ripen for some years. He included it in 1898 and again in 1899 in two of his lists of possible themes. But by the time he came to write the story, it had grown almost unbelievably from where it started. James' original intention, to be sure, had been to add to what he had been told such a different factor as that the man was really in love with another woman whom he wanted to marry after his divorce, and that he was employing the *cocotte* simply to shield this other woman from being compromised. Thus his first outline had already departed from the aspect of the situation that Zola, say, would have stressed, and had veered towards what, back in 1884, he had himself called, in skirting another situation of adultery, 'the characteristic manner of H. J.'

Frank Brivet, the hero of the completed story, has none of the tough earthiness of the American buccaneer who knows that he can buy anything he wants. His scruples are Jamesian; his purpose he finds, of course, 'sacred.' And Mrs. Dundene, the woman who helps him gain his end, is no *cocotte*. She serves at times as a model for the painter who tells the story, but, though she is not in society, she is a lady of the highest delicacy and tenderness. She has fallen hopelessly in love with Frank Brivet the first time she saw him in his friend's studio. She knows that his interest is all in Mrs. Cavenham, but she will sacrifice herself without a murmur. At the end, when he tells her that he will give her whatever present she wants, she chooses a portrait of him. Even that will bring him closer than he was in actuality, since, during all the alleged affair that secured him his freedom, she says, in the concluding line of the story, she 'never saw him alone.' To such a degree has Mrs. Dundene become a special type that the human nature of all concerned has been etherealized away.

James recognized that this story was not among his successes, for he left it out of his collected edition. *A Round of Visits* was one of the five stories that composed *The Finer Grain* (1910), all the short fiction he wrote after his collected edition had appeared. This story went through a development opposite to that of *The Special Type*. It started, not from a concrete anecdote, but as a Hawthornesque abstraction. James wrote in his notebook in the winter of 1894: 'There came to me a night or two ago the notion of a young man (young presumably) who has something—some secret sorrow, trouble, fault—to *tell* and can't find the recipient.' In that spring he added: 'There is apparently something worth thinking of in the idea I barely noted, a few weeks ago, of the young man with something on his mind.' He then continued for several hundred words, reaching towards the situation that as the young man goes with his misery from person to person, he finds each taken up with his own affairs. 'So he wanders, so he goes—with his burden only growing heavier—looking vainly for the ideal sympathy, the waiting, expectant, responsive, recipient. My little idea has been that he doesn't find it; but that he encounters instead a sudden appeal, an appeal more violent, as it were, more pitiful even than his own . . .'

James resumed this theme in his list of 1898, but a year later again he was still puzzling over how to handle it. He pictured anew the young man's isolation in London, 'in the great heartless preoccupied city,' and then wrote: 'I had thought, for the point of this, of his being suddenly approached by some one who demands *his* attention for some dreadful complication or trouble—a trouble so much greater than his own, a distress so extreme, that he sees the moral: the balm for his woe residing not in the sympathy of some one else, but in the coercion of giving . . . sympathy to some one else. I see this, however, somehow, as obvious and banal, *n'est-ce pas?*—"goody" and calculable beforehand. There glimmers out some better alternative, in the form of his making some one *tide over* some awful crisis by listening to him. He learns afterwards what it has been—I mean the crisis, the *other's* preoccupation, danger, anguish. (The thing needs working out—*maturing*.)'

By the time it had matured—several years later—James cast it, not in London, but in New York. He had written, particularly in *The Princess Casamassima,* many affecting passages about the crushing weight that London could be to the lonely individual. But he was now stimulated to record a new impression, the incredible world of the vast American hotel, as he had been exposed to it on his travels. Mark Monteith has returned to America after some few years' absence, to learn, on his arrival, that his friend Phil Bloodgood, to whom he had entrusted the management of his finances, has just absconded as a swindler. At the same

time, in the fierce New York blizzard, he falls sick with
grippe, and finds himself cooped up in the Hotel Poca-
hontas. James notes that 'the rich confused complexion' of
the savage seems here to show through the 'paint and
patches' of a Du Barry; he ends by imagining the *de luxe*
hotel as an enormous and oppressive jungle. As Monteith
crawls about it in his convalescence, he feels as though he
was threading a labyrinth: 'passing from one extraordinary
masquerade of expensive objects, one portentous "period"
of decoration, one violent phase of publicity, to another:
the heavy heat, the luxuriance, the extravagance, the quantity, the colour, gave the impression of some wondrous
tropical forest, where vociferous, bright-eyed and feathered
creatures, of every variety of size and hue, were half smothered between undergrowths of velvet and tapestry and
ramifications of marble and bronze. The fauna and the
flora startled him alike, and among them his bruised spirit
drew in and folded its wings.'

James is thoroughly cognizant of the economic basis of
such an overstuffed interior, of the pointless and appalling
waste.[2] When Monteith, driven by the need to talk over

[2] As another instance of how James' taste was his most accurate
register of social criticism, consider the judgment he gave—through
Densher's glimpse of Mrs. Lowder's 'treasures'—of the curiously mixed
state of mind we now call Victorian: 'It was only manifest they were
splendid and were furthermore conclusively British. They constituted
an order and abounded in rare material—precious woods, metals, stuffs,
stones. He had never dreamed of anything so fringed and scalloped,
so buttoned and corded, drawn everywhere so tight and curled everywhere so thick. He had never dreamed of so much gilt and glass, so
much satin and plush, so much rosewood and marble and malachite.
But it was above all the solid forms, the wasted finish, the misguided
cost, the general attestation of morality and money, a good conscience
and a big balance.'

his disaster, ventures outside to look up old friends, it is like 'a jump from the Tropics to the Pole.' Throughout the story James keeps us conscious both of the brutal bleakness of the city and of the shrill heartlessness of the protected, plumaged women whom Monteith calls upon, and who in their clatter about themselves fail even to notice that he is in trouble. Driven back upon himself and into the depths of depression, he hears that Newton Winch, a former acquaintance of Law School days, has also been down with the grippe, and has asked to be remembered to him. Catching at any straw, Monteith decides to pay him a visit, though he recalls Winch as being entirely ordinary and common.

He finds him transformed. Winch is nervous and sensitive, and after one look at his visitor's face, he knows that Monteith has had a bad shock. Winch encourages him to talk, and volunteers that of all Bloodgood's associates Monteith was the man of delicacy and confidence who would suffer most from his treachery. As they talk, an image of unexpected horror rises for Monteith. He thinks not of himself, but of Bloodgood: 'It was as if a far-borne sound of the hue and cry, a vision of his old friend hunted and at bay, had suddenly broken in.' And in another moment he becomes conscious of still another level of suffering beyond his own. What, indeed, can the maturing of Newton Winch be due to other than such suffering? Then, by means of James' characteristic introduction of a single unexplained concrete detail—'the tiny flash of a reflexion from fine metal, under the chair'—the whole complex situation is brought to its dramatic point. Winch is as deeply involved in larceny as Bloodgood, and while Monteith has been reflecting on what Bloodgood must be going through, Winch has had before his eyes an image of the misery his own conduct has likewise caused.

The apartment bell rings, and his host gestures to Monteith to answer it, knowing that the police must be there. Taking advantage of the moment of Monteith's absence, he recovers the pistol and shoots himself. Such an ending breaks the situation to pieces rather than resolves it, but what James achieved here was at the opposite pole from the ethical tenuosities and withdrawals of *The Special Type*. He had penetrated into a world so corrupted by money that the only escape seemed to be by violence.

The various shocks of American life had energized James just as he had hoped they would. Once he had finished his book of impressions, he was taken up with the project of selecting and collecting his works into twenty-four volumes for the New York edition, and with writing prefaces for them that would constitute 'a sort of comprehensive manual or *vademecum*' for aspirants to the art of fiction. The revision, particularly of the earlier novels, proved more of a task than he had bargained for,[3] and the job stretched out for over two years. Before he had quite finished it, he was writing to Howells, in the summer of 1908, of his 'impatience and yearning to get back . . . to too dreadfully postponed and neglected "creative" work,' since 'an accumulated store of ideas' was clogging his brain. 'I never have had such a sense of almost bursting, late in the day though it be, with violent and lately too repressed creative (again!) intention.' Such was his abundance in his

[3] For the extent of his work on *The Portrait of a Lady*, see the Appendix

mid-sixties, even though he described himself to another friend as the 'corpulent, slowly-circulating and slowly-masticating' master of Lamb House.

A return of the 'theatric dream' had already caused him to rewrite one of his old plays, *Covering End,* for Forbes Robertson, who brought it to the stage for a short run under the title of *The High Bid*—though it was crowded out by Jerome K. Jerome's *The Passing of the Third Floor Back.* During the following year he produced all the stories for *The Finer Grain;* but what he was most filled with at the opening of 1909 was that he had 'broken ground on an American novel.' As he again wrote to Howells: 'I find our art, all the while, more difficult of practice, and want, with that, to do it in a more and more difficult way; it being really, at bottom, only difficulty that interests me.'

This plan for *The Ivory Tower* was to be interrupted by more than a year of nervous ill health. Then, before he was finally recovered, came the great blow of William's death. Since his youngest brother Robertson had died only a few months previously, and his other brother and his sister many years before that, Henry was now left as the last of his immediate family. He turned instinctively to his memories. In some notes for *The American Scene,* he had already felt the older New England beckoning him, and had seen in particular Cambridge 'of the far-off unspeakable past years . . . like a pale pathetic ghost . . . fixing me with tender, pleading eyes, eyes of such exquisite pathetic appeal, and holding up the silver mirror just faintly dim, that is like a sphere peopled with the old ghosts.' He reached back to his New York beginning to memorialize, in his self-effacing autobiographical volumes, first his father and then William. Henry Adams' reaction to *Notes of a Son and Brother* was to dwell on the encroaching gloom of futility that seemed now wholly to surround their old age.

But James took an entirely different view. Answering Adams' letter in the spring of 1914, he made a magnificent confession of faith for a man nearing seventy-one. 'I have your melancholy outpouring . . . and I know not how better to acknowledge it than by the full recognition of its unmitigated blackness. *Of course* we are lone survivors, of course the past that was our lives is at the bottom of an abyss—if the abyss *has* any bottom; of course, too, there's no use talking unless one particularly *wants* to. But the purpose, almost, of my printed divagations was to show you that one *can*, strange to say, still want to—or can at least behave as if one did . . . I still find my consciousness interesting—under *cultivation* of the interest . . . You see I still, in presence of life (or of what you deny to be such), have reactions—as many as possible—and the book I sent you is a proof of them. It's, I suppose, because I am that queer monster, the artist, an obstinate finality, an inexhaustible sensibility. Hence the reactions—appearances, memories, many things, go on playing upon it with consequences that I note and "enjoy" (grim word!) noting. It all takes doing—and I *do*. I believe I shall do yet again—it is still an act of life.'

The Ivory Tower was to have been one of the most vigorous of these acts. He was at work on it again at last. In the form that we have it, it consists of three of the planned ten books and the opening of the fourth. James also left a preliminary draft of twenty-thousand words, outlining his

intention. He introduces a larger cast of characters than
had been his later practice, and he projects them at once
against a very sharply etched Newport background. This
again was a result of his recent travels, since he had been
deeply impressed with the transformation of the Newport
of his youth. He had figured this, in *The American Scene,*
in the image of 'a little bare, white, open hand' suddenly
crammed with gold. The old Newport of leisure and criticism and a sense of Europe had been obliterated by the
gigantic villas, 'all cry and no wool, all house and no garden,' a crowded row of 'white elephants' which already
stood as 'monuments to the *blasé* state of their absent pro-
prietors.'

In his novel he peopled them for their brief season. The
opening page presents Mr. Betterman's florid 'cottage,'
'smothered in senseless architectural ornament.' But the
most typical product of the scene is not the dying millionaire, but the middle-aged Bradhams—Davey and Gussy.
Davey sports a pristine version of the Harvard 'crew cut,'
his 'dense dark hair cropped close to his head after the
fashion of a French schoolboy or the inmate of a jail,' and
his face is 'lined and scratched and hacked across much in
the manner of the hard ice of a large pond at the end of a
long day's skating.' Davey is not vicious, but only 'a regu-
lar sponge of saturation in the surrounding medium.' His
wife Gussy is much less attractive: 'she was naturally never
so the vulgar rich woman able to afford herself all luxuries
as when she was most stupid about the right enjoyment of
these and most brutally systematic . . . for some inferior
and desecrating use of them.' James' adjectives are not
muffled here in his special aura, and they have caught like-

nesses that still look out at us each week from the society columns of the New York *Herald Tribune*.

The Bradhams are not the central characters, but they set the tone. As Mr. Betterman declares, 'Money is their life.' James reminded himself in his notes that such characters are essentially 'predatory'; and he introduced a terrifying image of a bird of prey in the first chapter, where Abel Gaw, another old millionaire, the associate and enemy of Frank Betterman's money-making years, hovers around his piazza, waiting for him to die. The renewed challenge that the dazzling dry American air had been to James' pictorial sense is attested by the extraordinary portrait that he develops here. All of Abel Gaw's intense financial rapacity is now contracted to the size of a 'little huddled figure' in a basket-chair, in whom the only sign of life is the incessant nervous movement of 'one small protrusive foot,' silhouetted against the sun and the sea. Such a portrait is as spare and telling in its gestures as Steichen's devastating study of the elder Morgan. And as Rosanna Gaw watches her father, she can think only that he perches there 'like a ruffled hawk, motionless but for his single tremor, with his beak, which had pecked so many hearts out, visibly sharper than ever, yet only his talons nervous.' Retired, aimless now, without any resources within himself, he is absorbed in the empty question of finding out at last how much old Frank had profited from the swindle that had broken them apart 'in hate and vituperation.'

Rosanna is in complete contrast to both her father and her surroundings. In the way that, as we have noted, James' later characters tend to go deeply back into his early experience, Rosanna is a recreation of Catherine Sloper, the

heroine of *Washington Square* (1880). That book, despite
its slightness, is so accurate in its human values that its
omission from James' collected edition is the one most to
be regretted. Those values are concentrated in the simple
moral goodness of Catherine, in contrast to the cruel egotism of her father and the bare-faced venality of her suitor.
In both Catherine and Rosanna, James has foregone the
attraction of obvious charms. Both are heavy placid young
women. As James remarks of Rosanna, there is 'a great deal
of her': she represents 'quantity and mass,' and her amplitude is 'essentially unobservant of forms,' which she never
found quite to fit her. As she says of herself, she was 'huge
and hideous' as a girl. She was, in brief, as unlike Daisy
Miller as she could possibly be. In her early thirties now,
her 'reality and sincerity' are striking in a society so lacking in them.

The situation that has been precipitated by Mr. Betterman's illness is the return from Europe of his nephew,
Graham Fielder. Years before when the boy was being
brought up abroad by his mother, Mr. Betterman had
urged him to come back. But Rosanna, though only six-
teen at the time, had already loathed her own wealth
and had taken a persuasive stand against his uncle's 'cruel
proposition' to involve Graham in 'the dreadful American
money world.' Summoned again now, he has come, not because his Europeanized culture really craves the inheritance, but 'simply to avoid a possible ugliness in his not
coming.' The interview between uncle and nephew is the
first climactic scene in the novel.

Fielder has had the sensation that his unexpected renewal of contact with the American world was as though

he was participating in a fairy-tale or a legend. It was just as if he was stepping 'into the chariot of the sun.' His uncle, in his 'beautiful bland dignity' might almost be a benevolent Olympian. For, however ruthless an operator Mr. Betterman may have been in the past, James wants now to make—as suggested through his allegorical name— a thorough contrast between him and Mr. Gaw. While Fielder is taking him in 'as the biggest and most native American impression' he could possibly be exposed to, Mr. Betterman, on his side, is appraising his nephew like 'an important "piece," ' and is satisfied with what he sees. He is glad now that Fielder did not come back at that earlier time; glad, too, that his nephew knows nothing of the market, since, as he says, 'I've *been* business and nothing else in the world.' He has come to realize that the life surrounding him is 'full of poison,' and seems to believe that Fielder can now act upon that life as an emissary from a more enlightened realm. To his nephew's modest disclaimer of having capabilities for anything whatsoever, Mr. Betterman declares, 'The question isn't of your doing, but simply of your being.' Thus does their interview oddly re-enact once more the pattern of James' own early education.

The next step in Fielder's return is his call upon Rosanna, whom he has not seen since her visit to Europe so many years before, when she had urged him to stay there. James conceived another marked contrast between these two. Fielder finds Rosanna unchanged, except that there is 'more of her' than he had quite reckoned; she finds him 'enormously different,' the difference consisting in his thorough absorption of European forms. But she still has much to say to him. She understands why Mr. Betterman now feels as he does about his nephew, since the air that the millionaire had breathed all his life had, in these last years, 'more and more sickened him.' A dramatic concentration is given to their talk, since Mr. Gaw now also lies dying upstairs, the victim of a sudden stroke—though, in his daughter's view, he is really 'dying of twenty millions,' inasmuch as these have dried up his life to the point that he has nothing at last left 'to pay with.'

Thus Abel Gaw is not to have the satisfaction of outliving his old adversary. But to Fielder's surprise, Rosanna's father has left a long letter addressed to him. This letter is the occasion for the introduction of the novel's leading symbol, which, though originally a biblical phrase, bears here the connotation of Sainte-Beuve's term for the romantics' escape from the world. Rosanna, reluctant to thrust the letter upon Fielder, leads up to it by offering it to him encased in a memento, a gold cigar case 'of absurd dimensions.' 'What strange things,' Fielder thought, 'rich persons had!' But as he doesn't smoke cigars, he begs off, and chooses instead, at her insistence that he take something, 'the one piece in the room that presented an interest,' though it too is 'a wonder of wasted ingenuity'—a small Indian cabinet in the form of an ivory tower, in a drawer of which his document can rest.

Fielder knows very little of his uncle's past, but we may easily conceive what the letter contains: a denunciation of Mr. Betterman's earlier dealings, in a grim attempt to poison Fielder's mind against him. Fielder's putting it into the cabinet without even breaking the seal is a sign of his instinctive flinching from the brutalities of the moneyed world. When he adds, in a jocular tone, 'Doesn't living in an ivory tower just mean the most distinguished retirement? I don't want yet awhile to settle in one my-self—though I've always thought it a thing I should like to come to,' we are also given a glance ahead at the possible denouement.

This scene between Fielder and Rosanna brings us to the end of the second book. In the third, which was sketched rather than closely written, James introduces his foils, Hor-ton ('Haughty') Vint and Cissy Foy. In a society whose only standards are monetary, they are without property, and en-grossed in the pursuit of it. They would have liked to marry, but they are equally without illusions, or, as Haughty says, 'horribly intelligent.' This unblinking rec-ognition of their situation is, in James' view, 'the crudest and the most typical, the most "modern." ' If Vint, in his carefully sheathed boldness, is to be the opposite of Fielder, Cissy is to be in even more striking contrast with Rosanna. James' notes tell us that Cissy was designed to impress Fielder at first as the person in this Newport world 'the most European,' the only one capable of 'understanding him intellectually,' and of 'entering into his tastes.' 'With Rosanna he isn't going to communicate "intellectually," aesthetically . . . the least little bit: Rosanna has no more taste than an elephant; Rosanna is only *morally* elephan-tine, or whatever it is that is morally most massive and magnificent.'

Some of the aspects of Cissy's hidden relationship with Vint might seem to risk reduplication with that of Kate and Densher; but what James warned himself against was the danger of repeating in Cissy the figure of Charlotte

Stant. Cissy was again to be the 'exceptionally clever' poor girl, living more or less by the bounty of the rich; but James has given her an acid sharpness that he denied to Charlotte. She says that she loathes 'the American girl.' And when Vint jauntily remarks, 'We're all unspeakably corrupt,' she reveals a greater penetration than his, by looking ahead to how Fielder will finally see through them, and answering that, on the contrary, they are still of a crudity of 'innocence.'

By the next scene Mr. Betterman has died, and Fielder is the sole inheritor. What James planned was that his hero, painfully aware of his ignorance of how to proceed, should turn to Vint to manage his property for him. At first he is to be fascinated, even dazzled, by his new friend. Only gradually does he come to perceive that Vint is swindling him. James knew that he was facing himself with a difficult problem in having to make 'credible and consistent' such a 'particular extraordinary relation.' He wanted to show Vint of a mental and moral 'audacity,' and finally of a 'profoundly nefarious' character. But he wanted him also to be a mixture of good and bad, so that Fielder could have the haunted sense that the bad was in a fashion his, Fielder's, creation through having put such an easy temptation in the other's path.

By this time Fielder has begun to comprehend the strange new world into which he has been plunged. James foresaw a period when his hero would want to give away his money to public services, 'after the fashion of Rockefellers and their like.' But through another conversation with Rosanna, he was to gain a deepened sense of what he had become implicated in. For she conveys to him her feeling that her resources 'are so dishonoured and stained and blackened at their very roots' that it seems to her—as it would have to Hawthorne—that 'benevolence' can hardly 'purge' them, or 'make them anything but continuators, somehow or other, of the wrongs in which they had their origin.' James does not indicate in his notes what event was finally to force the crisis, to crystallize Fielder's own impression 'of the black and merciless things that are behind the great possessions.' We could hardly have a more telling phrase than that for James' particular sense of evil in this novel. When that sense strikes home to Fielder, he will be glad to let go his *damnosa hereditas,* and return to Europe.

The persuasiveness of such a conclusion would depend upon Fielder's character. In one of the final passages of his unfinished notes James revealed how much he hoped to symbolize through his hero. He said that he had 'always wanted to do an out and out non-producer, in the ordinary sense of non-accumulator of material gain.' Yet he wanted Fielder no less different from the people who are 'idle' in America than from the people who are 'busy' with their 'ferocious acquisition.' He recognized that he was dealing again with 'a very special case,' but he wanted him also to be specially 'fine.' He wanted 'to steer clear of the tiresome "artistic" associations hanging about the usual type of young Anglo-Saxon "brought up abroad"; though only indeed as far as they *are* tiresome.' In brief, such a leisured hero is to be James' final protest against the narrow tensions and competitions of American life. Fielder is not to have 'at all the sense of a vacuous consciousness' or of 'a so-called wasted' existence. Yet he hasn't

anything 'to show in the way of work achieved.' But James
envisions some kind of nebulously distant achievement for
him: 'Heaven forbid he should "paint"—but there glimmers before me the sense of the connection in which I can
see him as more or less covertly and waitingly, fastidiously
and often too sceptically, conscious of possibilities of
"writing." ' With so many cushioning reservations does
James provide for his hero's future.

But what is the significance of such a symbolic figure,
and what is really before him? He has found out the impossibility of Mr. Betterman's scheme that he should continue to live in America as a shining if mute example to
his countrymen of the better life. He has made his gesture
of repudiation, but—for what? He will live like Strether
by his imagination, but, unlike Strether's, nearly all of his
mature life still stretches ahead. James had hardly thought
into the implications of Fielder's career beyond the final
recognition scene of his novel. This was to take place with
Rosanna. For James, even if he had not come to loathe
'the American girl,' as Cissy Foy did, had now seen to the
end of the possibilities, not only of a Daisy Miller, but of
an Isabel Archer and a Milly Theale. In an extraordinary
passage in *The American Scene* he had let the American
girl deliver her swan song. Travelling by train down the
length of the coast to Florida, he had become more and
more conscious of the commercialization of our life, by
the degree to which it had been yielded into the ready
hands of the universal salesman. The one frail carrier of
culture in such a world had been, as he had long insisted,
the young girl, who was free of the business shackles which
confined her brothers and cousins, and who took her possi-

bilities resolutely into her own hands. But by now James saw the odds arrayed against her as hopeless, and let her pour out a long soliloquy: 'Falsely beguiled, pitilessly forsaken, thrust forth in my ignorance and folly, what do I know, helpless chit as I can but be, about manners or tone, about proportion or perspective, about modesty or mystery, about a condition of things that involves, for the interest and the grace of life, other forms of existence than this poor little mine—pathetically broken reed as it is, just to find itself all waving alone in the wind? How can I do *all* the grace, all the interest, as I'm expected to?—yes, literally all the interest that isn't the interest on the money. I'm expected to supply it all—while I wander and stray in the desert . . . Haven't I . . . been too long abandoned and too *much* betrayed? Isn't it too late, and am I not, don't you think, practically lost?'

In line with these reflections James created in Rosanna a very different and more mature kind of heroine. Whether or not Fielder's final illumination in his talk with her is to carry to the length of their marriage, James does not say. But he conceived of this scene as of 'a big and beautiful value,' and it would certainly have symbolized the union between form and spirit, between Fielder's aesthetic perception and her moral massiveness. Perhaps James would also have been able to imagine here a solution for both Rosanna's and Fielder's problems in a free and growing life of culture that had put aside the curse of great wealth.

But at the point where he broke off his narrative, James had only begun to sketch the relationship between Fielder and Vint. There are signs of great tiredness in the writing, and he hardly succeeded in making Fielder's first thoughts

about his money seem more than those of the softest dilettante. On the last page that he wrote, however, James
found the kind of image that could always bring his loose
reflections into the focus of his camera-eye. He found it,
once again, through his recent response to American architecture. Fielder has gone out on the lawn of the vast empty
'cottage' that is now his, and circling around it, he looks
at it 'more critically than had hitherto seemed relevant.'
He is suddenly overwhelmed by its 'unabashed ugliness.'
Then—using an analogy which reminds us that James had
seen only the clumsy first attempts of a new age—Fielder
is seized with terror, eying his house 'very much as he
might have eyed some monstrous modern machine, one
of those his generation was going to be expected to master,
to fly in, to fight in, to take the terrible women of the future out for airings in . . .'

VI

The Religion of Consciousness

The great question as to a poet or a novelist is, How does he feel about life? What, in the last analysis, is his philosophy? When vigorous writers have reached maturity, we are at liberty to gather from their works some expression of a total view of the world they have been so actively observing. This is the most interesting thing their works offer us. Details are interesting in proportion as they contribute to make it clear.—JAMES, on Turgenieff.

JAMES broke off *The Ivory Tower* because the modern age had sounded its first alarm in July, 1914. His sensitive antennae recorded at once an interpretation of what was happening. He had only a moment of shocked blankness that anything 'so infamous' could happen 'in an age that we have been living in and taking for our own as if it were of a high refinement of civilization—in spite of all conscious incongruities.' But then, as he contemplated England, he had 'the terrible sense' that 'the people of this country may well—by some awful brutal justice—be going to get something bad for the exhibition that has gone on so long of their huge materialized stupidity and vulgarity.' As he looked out upon the world in that August, he concluded: 'The plunge of civilization into the abyss of blood and darkness by the wanton feat of those two infamous autocrats is a thing that so gives away the whole long age during which we have supposed the world to be, with whatever abatement, gradually bettering, that to have to take it all now for what the treacherous years were all the while really making for and *meaning* is too tragic for any words.'

He had thanked God years before, at the time of the Dreyfus case, that he had 'no opinions'; and had said that he was 'more and more only aware of things as a more or less mad panorama, phantasmagoria and dime museum.' But that was never strictly true. He always had the sudden plunging opinions of the non-political man. He denounced 'the foul criminality' of our newspapers at the time of the Spanish War. He saw Theodore Roosevelt throughout his career as 'a dangerous and ominous jingo,' as 'the mere monstrous embodiment of unprecedented resounding Noise.' On the other hand, the English election fight of 1910 had revealed to him 'how ardent a Liberal' lurked beneath his 'cold and clammy exterior.'

The effect of the war was to renew for him his memories of 1861, and, though again on the sidelines, he felt that he was a man with a country once more. He gave himself heart and soul to the English cause, and devoted unstinted time to causes and charities. He visited wounded soldiers in hospitals and spoke about them with some of Whitman's feeling. He was writing presently about 'the *louche* and sinister figure of Mr. Woodrow Wilson, who seems to be *aware* of nothing.' He believed that he made an inevitable move in changing his citizenship after we took no immediate action upon the sinking of the *Lusitania*.

In Percy Lubbock's view, *The Ivory Tower* 'had to be laid aside—it was impossible to believe any longer in a modern fiction, supposed to represent the life of the day, which the great catastrophe had so belied.' In the light of

that book's insight into the corruptions of the day, that
seems an extraordinarily shallow view. It might better be
said that the war made it even more impossible to imagine
a future for Graham Fielder. At all events the dissipations
of his time kept James from the concentration necessary to
work out the difficult problems of that novel, a novel
which, through the variety of its characters alone, seemed
likely to have measured up with his greatest. He turned to
other, less exacting tasks, to *The Sense of the Past,* and to
the continuation of his autobiography in *The Middle Years.*
But the many drains on his energy proved too great, and
he died early in 1916, before he could complete either of
these. In retrospect it seems sad that he allowed himself
to be so distracted from his proper work. Many others
could have done his jobs of bolstering morale. No one
else could add a sentence to his three unfinished works.

But he felt himself 'sick beyond cure' to have lived on
to see the 'black and hideous' wreckage of his age. *The
Sense of the Past* constituted a mode of escape. He had
thought of it first as long ago as the summer of 1900 when
Howells had been wanting another story of 'terror' like
The Turn of the Screw, and had suggested an 'international ghost.' But James had quickly seen that he couldn't
manage what he wanted within the prescribed limit of fifty
thousand words, and had laid the theme aside for a better
occasion. When he returned to it at last, he produced a
mood of eeriness rather than of terror.

His New York hero, Ralph Pendrel, has, at thirty, in-
herited unexpectedly a house in London, on the expiration
of the English branch of his family. His life up until now
has been 'mainly in the form of loss and of sacrifice,' but

as the author of a 'remarkable' *Essay in Aid of the Reading of History,* he will expose to Europe a 'prepared sensibility' very like James' own. Aurora Coyne, whom he would like to marry and take with him, has just returned from abroad. She has more vitality than he has. She resembles 'some great portrait of the Renaissance,' and, as he reflects sadly, he is 'a mere thinker,' whereas she would have liked a despot or a condottiere or even a pirate like Paul Jones. She says herself that she has come home to stay for good and that the man she will marry must be one who has made everything out of American experience. He calls this 'the new cry,' 'the new pose' of 1910, and asks sarcastically whether the question of 'the best we can turn out quite by ourselves' isn't settled by the cowboy. But he fails to persuade her.

The bulk of the novel—and it was more than half written—takes place in London. Pendrel brought to his first impressions the same breathless exhilaration that James recounted of himself in *The Middle Years,* going back to the time when he had parted from Minny Temple and had come abroad to write. Indeed, the description of the tourist's excitement over his first English breakfast is virtually the same in both books. But Pendrel carried his absorption in his old house to the length of wanting to identify himself with its life. He felt that by his 'deepening penetration' he could recover at least the simpler time of a century ago, 'the very tick of the old stopped clocks.' And wasn't recovering the lost very like 'entering the enemy's lines to get back one's dead for burial?' Hovering in his still unoccupied house late one evening, he finally makes his transference. He has the consciousness of exchanging places with the figure in the portrait of his early nineteenth-century ancestor—to such an extent were Hawthorne's devices to serve James to the end.

What follows is a prolonged *tour de force* both for Pendrel and for James. Pendrel can participate in that former world only by 'growing his perceptions' from moment to moment, and can thus serve as the final extension of James' method of suggesting the formation of his characters' thoughts. Surrounded by his family of that earlier time, he can know his situation only as he enacts it, and he always trembles on the verge of being found out. The fascination for James was that here he could portray a character with a complete double awareness of the past and of himself watching it, of 'the experience within the experience.' So far as he went James developed a contrast between 'the fierce characters and stronger passions' of Pendrel's roast-beef ancestors and his hero's somewhat attenuated if delicate sensibility. James planned to rescue him at the end. Pendrel is to begin to be homesick for his own time, for its 'ripeness and richness.' He is to develop a haunting fear that he may not be able to get back into the present again. In the meantime, Aurora is to experience a growing unrest, 'her own New York malaise.' She comes to London, and aided by the Ambassador, whom James based on his devoted memories of Lowell, she is to rescue Pendrel from his hallucination. James said that he planned only to prefigure their 'reunion, not to say union.' They will bring together the taste for the modern and the sense of the past; but once again the hanging garden of their future together is left symbolically indefinite.

The one quality of James' best work in such a *tour de*

force is the way he lets us share in his hero's excited consciousness of discovering, in the very nick of time, the reactions appropriate to the unforeseeable situations into which
he is immersed. As Orage wrote shortly after James' death:
'James was in love with the next world, or the next state of
consciousness; he was always exploring the borderland between the conscious and the superconscious.' The projection of the superconscious was what attracted him to the
ghost story. As he said in his preface to *The Altar of the
Dead*, 'the "ghost story," as we for convenience call it, has
ever been for me the most possible form of the fairy tale.' In
such stories he sought an air of verisimilitude for the supernatural by contriving for 'the strange and sinister' to be
'embroidered on the very type of normal and easy.' The
culmination of these efforts had been *The Jolly Corner*
(1908), another response to his renewed knowledge of New
York, another kind of re-entry into the past.

Here James presented, in Spencer Brydon, a man in his
middle fifties who has been away from America for over
thirty years, and who returns at last to look after his small
property. In the eyes of his New York contemporaries he
has spent 'a selfish frivolous scandalous life,' with nothing
to show for it. He now senses in himself what he had formerly never suspected, a real flair for business, and begins
to wonder what he would have been like if he had stayed
here all his life. Would he have been 'one of those types
who have been hammered so hard and made so keen by
their conditions?' He finds himself brooding on this *alter
ego* as he visits his old house downtown on 'the jolly corner,' as he fondly describes it. The question becomes obsessive as he begins to haunt the now unoccupied house

at night, as though he was tracking down a ghost. Once again James' evocation of a house depends on his incredibly developed pictorial skills. This time he presents the interior almost entirely by means of the light shining in from the street-lamps through the half-drawn blinds of the high windows, gleaming across the polished floors, picking out the massive silver door knobs, and dissolving into dark pools in the vast recesses. After many vigils in this setting Brydon finally encounters his quarry, only to wish that he had not. As he descends the stairwell, there lurks beneath the fan-lights of the outer door a figure in full evening dress. But his hands are spread across his face, and, with the flash of revulsion of which James is such a master, Brydon suddenly sees that two of the man's fingers are gone. Those bare stumps are of a piece with the horror that strikes Brydon when the stranger drops his hands and confronts him with a face that is blatant and odious in its evil.

But the man is no stranger, though Brydon faints away at the sight of him. This is the man Brydon himself would have become through the tensions of American life. James has created the revulsion here more compellingly than he was to do even with Graham Fielder's, since, imaging a house that was unquestionably destined to be torn down soon to make way for apartments, he was drawing on a peculiarly intimate sense of his own past, on his memories of the leisurely old New York that he felt had been obliterated by the rising city.

This sense of loss is pervasive through James' latest work. It can be traced back, to be sure, to the outset of his career, to his essay on Turgenieff (1874), for instance,

an essay that helps define James' own aims even better than
his many critiques of Balzac and Flaubert. For James discovered several resemblances between American and Rus-
sian life, particularly in the artist's relation to social
change. Turgenieff struck him as being quite 'out of harmony with his native land—of having what one may call
a poet's quarrel with it. He loves the old, and he is unable
to see where the new is drifting. American readers will
peculiarly appreciate this state of mind; if they had a native novelist of a large pattern, it would probably be, in a
degree, his own.' Reflecting especially on *Fathers and Sons,*
James added: 'The fermentation of social change has
thrown to the surface in Russia a deluge of hollow pretensions and vicious presumptions, amid which the love
either of old virtues or of new achievements finds very
little gratification.'

James had frankly stated that Turgenieff's possession of
a considerable fortune had had much to do with the fine
quality of his work. It had given him leisure and privacy,
and had enabled him to develop his rich urbanity. Though
James never possessed anything like Turgenieff's wealth,
he was always comfortably off and could devote himself to
cultivating the same attributes that he valued in the Rus-
sian. By the end of his career he was even more convinced
that the imagination is a conserving force. To H. G. Wells'
statement that his own work was 'anarchic,' James answered, in 1912: 'You are essentially wrong about that! No
talent, no imagination, no application of art . . . is able
not to make much less for anarchy than for a continuity
and coherency much bigger than any disintegration.

There's no representation, no picture . . . that isn't by its
very nature preservation.'

But the question that forced itself was, What could the
imagination preserve? Not in James' case, as he had long
been ruefully aware, anything like the social solidity and
wholeness that he had admired especially in Balzac. James
never knew enough about his changing America for that.
Nor, it must be repeated, had the older America developed
anything like the intricate structure that the French novelist could record. What it came down to for James was
the preservation, not of a sense of society, but of a sense
of personal relations.

Some of his ghosts suggest how difficult it was for him
at times to preserve even that. His notebooks record with
a compulsive frequency such themes as that of the girl
'whose husband is to show her everything,' and who therefore waits to begin experience with her marriage. But she
never gets a husband, or rather, 'the husband comes in the
form of death.' Or again James asked himself: 'What is
there in the idea of *too late*—of some friendship or passion
or bond—some affection long desired and waited for?' He
dwelt on the passions 'that might have been.' He knew that
'the wasting of life is the implication of death.' He worked
out such themes in *The Friends of the Friends* (1896) and
The Beast in the Jungle (1903). But in *Maud-Evelyn*
(1900) he overreached himself, and wrote a story that is
ghastly in a sense he did not intend. The hero falls in love
with the photograph of a dead girl, and urged on by her
parents who live entirely in their memories, he goes to the
length of believing that he is engaged to her, and finally
that he has married her and lost her. Such love for the

dead is saved from Poe's ghoulish extremes only by the girl's not coming back to life.

Graham Greene, writing out of his own intense sense of evil, has said that James' 'experience taught him to believe in supernatural evil, but not in supernatural good.' Too much can hardly be made of the chief evidence that Greene cited, of the ineradicable mark that must have been left on James' consciousness by the fact that both his father and his brother had undergone shattering visions of horror. Each recorded his vision, and in each we enter a realm of obsessive dread akin to that probed in *The Turn of the Screw*. The father's experience, which he came to refer to as a vastation, occurred when Henry was a year old: 'Towards the close of May, having eaten a comfortable dinner, I remained sitting at the table after the family had dispersed, idly gazing at the embers in the grate, thinking of nothing, and feeling only the exhilaration incident to a good digestion, when suddenly—in a lightning-flash as it were—"fear came upon me, and trembling, which made all my bones to shake." To all appearances it was a perfectly insane and abject terror, without ostensible cause, and only to be accounted for, to my perplexed imagination, by some damned shape squatting invisible to me within the precincts of the room, and raying out from his fetid personality influences fatal to life. The thing had not lasted ten seconds before I felt myself a wreck, that is, reduced from a state of firm, vigorous joyful manhood to one of almost helpless infancy.' At the end of an hour he had regained his self-possession to the point of being able to call to his wife and communicate his state to her. But he had lost all confidence in his self-hood, indeed he had come to believe that self-hood is 'the curse of mankind.' He was to find his way back to mental health slowly, through his conversion to Swedenborgianism. He never lost the belief which he acquired during that breakdown and later expressed in his book on *The Nature of Evil,* that 'the fall is self-sufficiency.' That is why he kept urging his sons, as Henry noted, that 'we need never fear not to be good enough if we were only social enough.' That is also why he called his final work *Society the Redeemed Form of Man* and argued there again that the origin of evil springs wholly from having self-consciousness instead of social consciousness.

Writing to William shortly after their father's death in 1882, Henry had reflected, 'how intensely original and personal his whole system was, and how indispensable it is that those who go in for religion should take some heed of it.' But he had to say that he could not enter into it much himself, that he could not be so theological. He had felt inescapably closer to William's problems, and the crisis that had almost broken William's life impinged upon his own most matured sense of evil, and can help finally to define that sense as it pervades so many of his stories.

The seizure which William was to describe in his *Varieties of Religious Experience* had descended upon him at the beginning of the eighteen-seventies, in that period which had been so uncertain for them both. While in a state 'of philosophic pessimism and general depression,' he had gone 'one evening into a dressing-room in the twilight to procure some article which was there; when suddenly there fell upon me without any warning, just as if it came out of the darkness, a horrible fear of my own existence.

Simultaneously there arose in my mind the image of an epileptic patient whom I had seen in the asylum, a black-haired youth with greenish skin, entirely idiotic . . . This image and my fear entered into a species of combination with each other. *That shape am I,* I felt, potentially. Nothing that I possess can defend me against that fate, if the hour for it should strike for me as it struck for him. There was such a horror of him, and such a perception of my own momentary discrepancy from him, that it was as if something hitherto solid within my breast gave way entirely and I became a mass of quivering fear. After this the universe was changed for me altogether.'

He was haunted for months by 'a horrible dread' of 'the pit of insecurity beneath the surface of life . . . The fear was so invasive and powerful that if I had not clung to scripture-texts like "The eternal God is my refuge," etc., "Come unto me, all ye that labor and are heavy-laden," etc., "I am the resurrection and the life," etc., I think I should have grown really insane.' But unlike his father, he found his way out through philosophy rather than through religion. The first insight that steadied him was Renouvier's definition of Free Will: 'the sustaining of a thought *because I choose to* when I might have other thoughts.' He determined to act on that as if it was not an illusion and declared: 'My first act of free will shall be to believe in free will.' From there he carried through to his own meliorism and optimism, and finally belonged, to use his own categories, with the healthy and not the sick-minded. But while the crisis was still close to him, he had written Henry: 'It seems to me that all a man has to depend on in this world, is, in the last resort, mere brute power of resistance. I can't bring myself, as so many men seem able to, to blink the evil out of sight, and gloss it over. It's as real as the good, and if it's denied, good must be denied too.'

Henry was hardly more of a philosopher than he was a theologian, even though, as we have seen, he was concerned, particularly in the cases of Isabel Archer and of Strether, with what Strether called 'the illusion of freedom.' But, even though he continued to read his brother's works 'with rapture,' and declared, upon the appearance of *Pragmatism* (1907), that he was 'lost in the wonder of the extent to which all my life I have (like M. Jourdain) unconsciously pragmatised,' he had scarcely the trace of a system. Spectator rather than either doer or thinker, he had proceeded to compose and to frame the most glittering scenes. But in a more enduring way than either his father or his brother had done, he kept throughout life the sense of the abyss always lurking beneath the fragile surface. He expressed this kind of evil, again and again, through a long series of characters. This was what Maggie Verver had called 'the horror of the thing hideously *behind,* behind so much trusted, so much pretended, nobleness, cleverness, tenderness,' and what Graham Fielder had sensed as 'the black and merciless things that are behind the great possessions.'

Yet, curiously enough, the passage in his own works that is most akin to the record of a personal hallucination expresses, in a fantasy of escape, a sense of supernatural good rather than of supernatural evil. In *The Great Good Place* (1900) George Dane, an elderly writer exhausted by too much work, oppressed by a desk piled high with too many unanswered letters, collapses on his sofa, only to have the sensation of awakening in a 'broad deep bath of stillness.' He has kept 'the blest fact of consciousness,' but everything else is changed. In the beautiful cloister in which he finds himself it is as though he had entered 'some mild Monte Cassino, some Grande Chartreuse more accessible.' Or rather it is a retreat for pressure-ridden Protestants, who have no retreats of their own, a refuge for 'the sensitive individual case.' As Dane tries to figure its quality further, he can approach it only through a series of comparisons, each of which strikes him as inadequate. It is like a country house or even a club, though it is also a bath and a cure. It's very expensive and yet it's 'liberty hall.' His most prevalent sensation is that of 'leaning back on the cushion and feeling a delicious ease.' But when a companion suggests the analogy of a convalescent home, he demurs and finds a more satisfying likeness in 'some great mild invisible mother who stretches away into space and whose lap's the whole valley . . .' Out of his complete relaxation he wakes again on his own sofa, to find that he has slept through the entire day, while a younger friend has reduced the mountain on his desk.

A fantasy of another world cast so overwhelmingly in the luxury products of this one betrays the vulgarity into which James could fall through the very dread of being vulgar. His prolonged insistence that 'there is every form of softness in the great good place' ends by giving us a sickening sensation of everything that is least virile in his imagination. Such a fantasy sprang from his uprooted religious sense which had been deprived in childhood of any normal development. His father's desire that his sons should be exposed to the range of possibilities had caused them to attend every kind of church in turn. The result for William was that he could finally anatomize the varieties of religious experience as being somehow all equal, and equally uncompelling. But Henry said that even as a boy he had felt 'a certain sophistry' in their having the freedom of all churches. It had struck him finally as an embarrassing freedom, and he had come to wish that 'we might have been either much less religious or much more so.' In the vague contours of his father's Swedenborgianism Henry felt most of all the need for some form that would make the religious life coherent, but 'there was not an item of the detail of devotional practice that we had been so much as allowed to divine.

Greene, a Catholic convert himself, believes that James was moving towards a deeper sympathy with Catholicism. It is true that James described the Catholic Church as 'the most impressive convention in all history.' It is also true that, from Rowland Mallet to Strether, James' Americans find relief and solace in European cathedrals. But it remains equally true that, for Strether, Notre Dame 'had no altar for his worship, no direct voice for his soul'; and James' characters, even Densher when he visits the Oratory on that Christmas morning shortly after Milly's death, never go beyond hovering before the altars of the dead.

James' religion was phrased very accurately by Eliot as an 'indifference to religious dogma' along with an 'exceptional awareness of spiritual reality.' It is likely that a man of James' sensibility, if his mind had been formed in our age of crisis, would have felt, as Eliot has, the ineluctable necessity of religious order. But James himself left a

statement of his matured religious beliefs in a seldom-read
essay, *Is There a Life After Death?* This was his contribution to the kind of symposium in which the America of
1910 took satisfaction. Borrowing its title, *In After Days,*
from a refrain of Austin Dobson's, and appearing in a
binding of light violet, it was led off by Howells and concluded by James, with Julia Ward Howe, Thomas Went-
worth Higginson, and several others in between. What
James had to say may not be important as a contribution
to speculations on immortality, but it gives his most un-
impeded expression of his final values in this world.

As he contemplated death, it could produce one of two
effects upon his spirit: it could make him desire it either
'as welcome extinction and termination,' or 'as a renewal
of the interest, the appreciation, the passion, the large and
consecrated consciousness, in a word, of which we have had
so splendid a sample' in our life here. The formulation is
characteristic in that for his old age both alternatives
pointed to a desire and not to a dread, and in that so
many of his especially valued words already indicate to
which alternative he inclined. As he proceeded, he brought
into play the same standards by which he judged the characters in his novels. They always fell into their positions
on his scale according to their degree of awareness: the
good character was the one who was most sensitive, who
saw the greatest variety of moral possibilities, and who
wanted to give them free play in others. The bad character was obtuse or willfully blind to such possibilities; he
was dead in himself, and, at his self-centered worst, tried
to cause the spiritual death of others.

So too in James' discussion of immortality: 'the quantity or quality of our practice of consciousness' in this world 'may have something to say to it.' Looking around him at 'all the ugliness, the grossness, the stupidity, the cruelty,' he read therein the record of 'the so easy non-existence of consciousness,' and sadly took it for granted that 'for the constant and vast majority' life yields nothing in the way of 'intelligible suggestion.' His father had argued that 'Divine truth has first to create the intelligence it afterwards enlightens,' but he had believed more confidently in humanity's capacity for social redemption. His son's conception of grace was aristocratic, and he was virtually to say: 'The soul is immortal certainly—if you've got one—but most people haven't.'

Perhaps too much has been made recently of James' stress on evil and on suffering. He contemplated the facts of decay and wastage, of incessant and insufferable loss, and yet pitted against these his feeling, as he grew older, of the ever richer accumulations of experience. Indeed, he based his hope for immortality on the intensity of his desire for it. He argued that it was senseless to assume that just as an individual had been granted his final ripening, just as he had attained 'this beautiful and enjoyable independence of thought,' he should then be snuffed out in 'complete privation.' His argument for survival is loosely neo-Platonic. As he had written to William long ago, at the time of Minny's death: 'The more I think of her, the more perfectly satisfied I am to have her translated from this changing realm of fact to the steady realm of thought.'

Now, in his old age, he had the feeling that beyond all the phases and aspects of his long career of observation there lay far other combinations and patterns, that all his life so far had given him just a glimpse of 'the unlimited vision of being.' He insists that he argues, not as a special type, but as 'the altogether normally hampered and benighted random individual.' Yet 'the renewal of existence' for which he longs is commensurate with the artist's endless cultivation of experience, since the artist beyond other men lives by means of 'immersion in the fountain of being.' As James repeats such a term as 'being,' as he arrives at his conclusion that consciousness has come to absorb him so much that he simply cannot believe that further gradations and developments do not lie ahead, he recognizes that his conception comes back, if oddly and obliquely, 'to the theory of the spiritual discipline, the purification and preparation on earth for heaven, of the orthodox theology.' But he knows too that the resemblance is essentially superficial, since with all his desire to attain purer patterns of the mind, his values remain thoroughly mundane. He does not want to lose his personality in God, but to preserve it intact for further enrichment. As George Dane had said in *The Great Good Place*, 'I don't speak of the putting off of one's self; I speak only—if one has a self worth sixpence—of the getting it back.' James could reap the full advantages of the nineteenth-century liberalism of his father's generation and could rely on the supreme value of the unaided consciousness. When he projected this further and affirmed his belief in sanctions for immortality, he found these sanctions, as Proust was to do in his famous passage describing the death of Bergotte, in the essences of aesthetic idealism.

The consciousness which James dwells on 'as the highest good I can conceive of,' though interpenetrated with ethical values, is more of the mind than of the soul. James is not a spiritual writer in the sense that Hawthorne and Dostoevsky are. What fascinated and often bewildered the friends of his latest years was how the most casual question could set into motion all his mental resources, as though he felt it his obligation to examine what the mind of Henry James was in relation to every stimulus, no matter how accidental or trivial. He never lost his boyhood curiosity about the otherness of the outside world. He was, to the end, the absorbed spectator, and though he had noted how a character like Hyacinth Robinson could, through poverty, through being shut off from the world of his dreams, become a trapped spectator, such a character in James' fiction is the exception rather than the norm. It certainly did not occur to him that Graham Fielder might feel himself equally trapped, that the resources of sensibility, that the manifold delight in personal relations might come to seem both inadequate and excessive in a society whose decay was no longer hidden beneath the surface as it was to James' eyes through most of his career. Yet, as I have argued elsewhere, only a step, only a slight shift in attitude separated James' narrator in *The Sacred Fount* from the Tiresias of *The Waste Land,* who is fated to *see* everything that is enacted in that poem. Once the older society did seem utterly insecure, the exclusive concern with the interactions of a special group became a nightmare. And the observer, aware that he fulfilled no vital rôle, that he could leave no effectual mark on his surroundings, felt his consciousness no longer a blessing, as Strether felt it to be, but a torture, since it was 'doomed to foresuffer all' that passed before him in a sequence blindly without purpose.

James' father had supplemented Swedenborg with

Fourier, and had held finally that 'life is simply the passage of idea into action.' His philosophy embraced both religion and politics. He believed in a fusion of the spiritual and the social, not to the attenuation of either but for the reinforcement of both. Both the religious man and the political and economic man find inadequate the view of life expressed by his son. Yet James perceived what was lacking in his father's world. His father's concern with what was universal rather than with what was individual had diffused itself so widely that it ended by losing the image of any actual man. Hence James was impelled to believe that the primary obligation for the artist was to start with the tangible, with what he had seen for himself. And if his image of man is restricted, if it has little of the radiant aura of his father's or of Emerson's aspiration, it possesses the indispensable quality of mature art: it is compellingly concrete. Therefore, although James did not advance the empirical attitude with the simple vigor of his brother, the world portrayed in his novels is of substantial value to us in recharting our own world, if only by providing us with a target to shoot against.

The thinkers and the artists of the next generation are faced again with the problem that confronted James' father. Neither the economic man nor the religious man, so widely and so abstractly separated in most of our recent literature, now seems sufficient alone. James' father could count himself both a Christian and a democrat. James' brother was more of the second than the first, and all his social values were uncompromisingly equalitarian. James himself was neither the one nor the other. Yet he profited from the heritage of both, and it seems doubtful now

whether the humane consciousness that he expressed at
such a high point can survive in our world without a renewed synthesis of the sort that his father attempted. That
particular synthesis of Swedenborg and Fourier, to be sure,
is too expansive and too innocent to serve for much of a
foundation. James' own work is far more serviceable to us,
both in its depth and in its limitations. His intense spiritual awareness, drifting into a world without moorings, has
told others beside Eliot that if religion is to persist, it must
be based again in coherent dogma. At the opposite pole,
our novelists of social protest can still learn much, as
Robert Cantwell has incisively argued, from James' scale
of values. His gradation of characters according to their
degree of consciousness may be validly translated into terms
of social consciousness, and thus serve as a measure in a
more dynamic world than James ever conceived of. To
those who believe that if both Christianity and democracy
are to endure, the next synthesis must be more rigorously
based in both political economy and theology, in the theology that recognizes anew man's radical imperfection, and
in the radical political economy that insists that, whether
imperfect or not, men must be equal in their social opportunities, many of James' values are, oddly enough, not
at all remote.

The Painter's Sponge and Varnish Bottle

I

ONE SIGN of how little technical analysis James has received is the virtual neglect of his revisions. Beyond Theodora Bosanquet's sensitive remarks in 'Henry James at Work' and occasional citation to annotate the elaborations of his later manner, they have been passed by. The only detailed exception is an essay on *Roderick Hudson* wherein the writer held that James' additions had largely served to spoil the clean outlines of its style.[1] Yet James made these revisions at the plentitude of his powers, and they constituted a *re-seeing* of the problems of his craft. He knew that it would be folly to try to recast the structure of any of his works. In the first preface that he wrote, that to *Roderick Hudson,* he developed an analogy for his aims in the way his fellow-craftsman on canvas went about to freshen his surfaces, to restore faded values, to bring out 'buried secrets.' He undertook, in particular, a minute verbal reconsideration of the three early novels that he chose to republish.

My reason for singling out *The Portrait of a Lady* is that it is a much richer book than either of the two others.

[1] Hélène Harvitt, 'How Henry James Revised *Roderick Hudson:* A Study in Style,' PMLA (March 1924), 203-27.

Roderick Hudson is full of interest for James' development, since the two halves of his nature, the creator and the critic, are in a sense projected in Roderick and Rowland. Moreover, he there first tried out his device of having his narrative interpreted by the detached observer. But the book as a whole remains apprentice work. The revision of *The American*—the most extensive of all—might tell us, among other things, how James tried to repair what he had himself come to consider the falsely romantic aspects of his denouement. But *The Portrait of a Lady* is his first unquestioned masterpiece. By considering all the issues that the revisions raise, we may see it with renewed clarity.[2]

Larger changes are very few. A page of conversation between Ralph Touchett and Lord Warburton (at the very end of Chapter XXVII) was recast in a way that shows James' more mature sense of a dramatic scene. What had been two pages of psychological scrutiny of Osmond just before his proposal to Isabel (Chapter XXIX) were felt by James to be otiose, and were cut to ten lines—an item of interest for the conventional view that the older James always

[2] James had developed early the habit of touching up his texts wherever possible; and he even made a few slight alterations in the *Portrait* between its appearance in *The Atlantic Monthly* (November 1880—December 1881) and in volume form. For instance, Madame Merle's first name was changed from Geraldine to Serena. But the changes that can instruct us in the evolution of his technique are naturally those he introduced when returning to the book after more than a quarter of a century.

James' copies of both *The American* and *The Portrait of a Lady*, containing his innumerable revisions in longhand on the margins and in inserted pages of typescript, are now in the Houghton Library at Harvard.

I want to thank again the group of Harvard and Radcliffe students with whom I read through Henry James in the winter of 1943, since they did most of the spade work for this essay.

worked the other way. But, with two important exceptions later to be looked into, we are to be concerned here with the tiniest brush strokes. What must be kept constantly in mind, therefore, is the design of the canvas as a whole. If that is done, we may have the intimate profit of watching the artist at his easel and of gaining insight into his principles of composition.

The writer's equivalent for the single flake of pigment is the individual word; and two words which James felt to be in need of consistent readjustment—'picturesque' and 'romantic'—form in themselves an index to his aims. He had begun the book in Florence and had finished it in Venice. He had been at the time still strongly under the spell of Italian art, which, as he wrote William, had first taught him 'what the picturesque is.' He had consequently used the word freely as a kind of aesthetic catch-all, too loosely as he came to feel, for he struck it out in almost every case. He had applied it to Gardencourt, to Isabel's grandmother's house in Albany, to Osmond's *objets d'art;* he changed it in the first case to 'pictorial,' in the others to 'romantic.' [3] Some of its many other occurrences must have made the later James wince, especially where he had said that Madame Merle had 'a picturesque smile.' That was altered to 'amused.' It is significant that when the word was retained, it was qualified by the speaker, by Isabel, who says that she would be a little on both sides of a revolution, that she would admire the

[3] I have included all the detailed references to both editions in the version of this essay that appeared in *The American Bookman* (Winter 1944). To avoid spotting these pages with unnecessary footnotes, I refer to that periodical any reader who is interested in following out the comparison for himself.

Tories since they would have 'a chance to behave so exquisitely. I mean so picturesquely.' 'So exquisitely' was
added in the revision, and it is no accident that where, in
the earlier version, Lord Warburton had remarked that
Isabel found the British 'picturesque,' he was later made
to say ' "quaint." ' That putting into quotation marks underscores Isabel's attitude, as, indeed, do several instances
where James introduced 'romantic' not merely as a sub-
stitute for 'picturesque.' Isabel's first judgment of Caspar
as 'not especially good looking' becomes 'he was not ro-
mantically, rather obscurely handsome'; and her initial
response to Warburton as 'one of the most delectable persons she had met' is made much firmer—she judges him,
'though quite without luridity—as a hero of romance.' And
when we find that she doesn't tell her sister about either
his or Osmond's proposal, not simply because 'it entertained her to say nothing' but because 'it was more romantic,' and she delighted in 'drinking deep, in secret, of
romance,' we have the clue to what James is building up
through his greatly increased use of this adjective and
noun. He is bound to sharpen the reader's impression of
how incorrigibly romantic Isabel's approach to life is, an
important issue when we come to judge the effect of the
book's conclusion.

Another word that shows the drift of James' later concern is 'vulgar.' One of James' most limiting weaknesses,
characteristic of his whole phase of American culture, was
dread of vulgarity, a dread that inhibited any free approach to natural human coarseness. But here the increased
intrusion of the word does no great damage. When 'the
public at large' becomes 'a vulgar world,' or when Hen-

rietta Stackpole asserts that our exaggerated American stress on brain power 'isn't a vulgar fault' (she had originally pronounced it a 'glorious' one), or when Isabel adds to her accruing reflections that Osmond had married her, 'like a vulgar adventurer,' for her money, we simply see more sharply the negative pole of James' vision.

His positive values come out in a whole cluster of words affecting the inner life of his characters, words in which we may read all the chief attributes of Jamesian sensibility. Ralph's 'delights of observation' become 'joys of contemplation.' Warburton's sisters' 'want of vivacity' is sharpened to 'want of play of mind,' just as Isabel's 'fine freedom of composition' becomes 'free play of intelligence.' On the other hand, Warburton, in Ralph's description, is toned down from 'a man of imagination' to 'a man of a good deal of charming taste,' in accordance with the high demands that James came to put upon the imagination as the discerner of truth. It is equally characteristic that Isabel's 'feelings' become her 'consciousness,' and that her 'absorbing happiness' in her first impressions of England becomes 'her fine, full consciousness.' She no longer feels that she is 'being entertained' by Osmond's conversation; rather she has 'what always gave her a very private thrill, the consciousness of a new relation.' Relations, intelligence, contemplation, consciousness—we are accumulating the words that define the Jamesian drama. No wonder that James came to feel that it had been flat to say that Isabel was fond 'of psychological problems.' As he rewrote it, she became fond, as he was, 'ever, of the question of character and quality, of sounding, as who should say, the deep personal mystery.'

II

To progress from single words to questions of style, we note at once the pervasive colloquialization. The younger James had used the conventional forms, 'cannot' and 'she would'; in his revised conversation these always appear as 'can't' and 'she'd.' Of more interest is his handling of the 'he said—she said' problem, upon which the older James could well take pride for his ingenuity. Isabel 'answered, smiling' becomes Isabel 'smiled in return' or Isabel 'gaily engaged.' Osmond 'hesitated a moment' becomes that Jamesian favorite, Osmond 'just hung fire.' And for one more out of a dozen other evasions of the obvious, the Countess Gemini no longer 'cried . . . with a laugh'; her sound and manner are condensed into one word, 'piped.'

James' humor has often been lost sight of in discussion of the solemnities of his mandarin style. But he didn't lose it himself. His original thumb-nail characterization of Isabel's sister was descriptive: 'Lily knew nothing about Boston; her imagination was confined within the limits of Manhattan.' A graphic twist brings that to life with a laugh: 'her imagination was all bounded on the east by Madison Avenue.'

The later James was more concrete. He had also learned what a source of life inheres in verbal movement. 'Their multifarious colloquies' is heavily abstract, whereas 'their plunge . . . into the deeps of talk' takes us right into the action. So too with the diverse ways in which James launched his characters into motion, as when Henrietta 'was very well dressed' became 'she rustled, she shim-

mered'; or when the Countess, instead of entering the
room 'with a great deal of expression,' did it 'with a flut-
ter through the air.' Such movement means that James was
envisaging his scenes more dramatically; and, in the passage where Isabel has just been introduced to Osmond, we
can see how natural it had become, for the novelist to
heighten any theatrical detail. Where he had formerly
written that Isabel sat listening to Osmond and Madame
Merle 'as an impartial auditor of their brilliant discourse,'
he now substituted 'as if she had been at the play and
had paid even a large sum for her place.' And as this scene
advances, instead of saying that Madame Merle 'referred
everything' to Isabel, James wrote that she 'appealed to
her as if she had been on the stage, but she could ignore
any learnt cue without spoiling the scene.'

Operating more pervasively, here as always, upon James'
imagination, were analogies with pictures rather than with
the stage. When he wanted to enrich his bare statement
that the Countess 'delivered herself of a hundred remarks
from which I offer the reader but a brief selection,' he
said that she 'began to talk very much as if, seated brush
in hand before an easel, she were applying a series of con-
sidered touches to a composition of figures already sketched
in.' A phrase that shows us James' very process is when
Isabel, instead of 'examining the idea' (of Warburton's
'being a personage'), is made to examine 'the image so
conveyed.' The growth from ideas to images is what James
had been fumbling for in his earlier preoccupation with
the picturesque. The word might now embarrass him, but
not the secret he had learned through it. He had originally opened the first of the chapters to be laid in Os-

mond's villa by remarking that 'a picturesque little group'
was gathered there. What he meant to imply was made
much more explicit in the revision: 'a small group that
might have been described by a painter as composing
well.'

That concern with composition grew from the conviction which he voiced in the preface to *Roderick Hudson,*
that the novelist's subject, no less than the painter's, consisted ever in 'the related state, to each other, of certain
figures and things.' And characters, he came to believe,
could be best put into such relations when they were realized as visually, as lambently, as possible. This belief led
him into one of his most recurrent types of revision, into
endowing his *dramatis personae* with characterizing images.
He had concluded his initial account of Ralph's ill health
by remarking, 'The truth was that he had simply accepted
the situation.' In place of that James was to introduce the
poignancy that is Ralph's special note: 'His serenity was
but the array of wild flowers niched in his ruin.' In comparable fashion, James added to his first description of
Osmond, with no parallel in the original, an image that
embodies the complex nature we are to find in him: 'He
suggested, fine gold coin as he was, no stamp nor emblem
of the common mintage that provides for general circula-
tion; he was the elegant complicated medal struck off for
a special occasion.'

Such elaborate images, more than any other aspect of
James' later style, show his delight in virtuosity. Occasionally they seem to have been added purely because his eye
fell on a dull patch of canvas, and he set out to brighten it
up. Warburton's dim sisters don't contribute much in the

original beyond 'the kindest eyes in the world.' But, in revising, James let himself go: their eyes are now 'like the balanced basins, the circles of "ornamental water," set, in parterres, among the geraniums.' In that image any functional intention may seem lost in the rococo flourish; but such was not usually the case. Take one very typical instance in the first detailed description of Caspar Goodwood—and it is significant of James' matured intentions that he introduced characterizing images of his chief figures at such important points. We are told in the first version that Caspar had undergone the usual gentleman athlete's education at Harvard, but that 'later, he had become reconciled to culture.' In the revision James conveyed much more of Caspar's energetic drive by means of a muscular image: 'later on he had learned that the finer intelligence too could vault and pull and strain.'

The full effect that James was trying for in such images might be instanced by the chapter which introduces Henrietta. Here we might follow James in the process of enlivening his sketch by a dozen fresh touches. The most interesting of these bring out Henrietta's character by the device of interrelating her appearance with her career. He did not rest content with saying that 'she was scrupulously, fastidiously neat. From top to toe she carried not an inkstain.' He changed this into: 'she was as crisp and new and comprehensive as a first issue before the folding. From top to toe she had probably no misprint.' In spite of the loudness of her voice (which caused James to alter Henrietta 'murmured' to Henrietta 'rang out'), Ralph was originally surprised to find that she was not 'an abundant talker.' But in the revision the detailed glance at her profession is sustained, and he finds her not 'in the large type, the type of horrid "headlines." ' Yet she still remains fairly terrifying to Ralph, and, a few pages farther on, James emphasized that by another kind of image. To point up the fact that 'she was brave,' he added, 'she went into cages, she flourished lashes, like a spangled lion-tamer.' With that as a springboard James could rise to the final sentence of this chapter. Originally Ralph had concluded, 'Henrietta, however, is fragrant—Henrietta is decidedly fragrant!' But this became a punch line: 'Henrietta, however, does smell of the Future—it almost knocks one down!'

James remarked in his preface that he had given the reader 'indubitably too much' of Henrietta—a thing that could be said of most of his *ficelles;* but in retouching he had at least done what he could to brighten every inch. In relation to her we may note another phase of his revision, his addition of epithets to characterize the world of which she is part. In Rome she is struck by the analogy between the ancient chariot ruts and 'the iron grooves which mark the course of the American horse-car.' These become more up to date: 'the overjangled iron grooves which express the intensity of American life.' Where James had written 'the nineteenth century,' he was later to call it 'the age of advertisement'; and glancing, not at America but at Europe, he named it 'an overcivilized age.' But it was Henrietta's realm he was thinking of again when, instead of having Madame Merle remark that 'it's scandalous, how little I know about the land of my birth,' he had her call it rather, in his most revelatory addition of this type: 'that splendid, dreadful, funny country—surely the greatest and drollest of them all.'

III

So far I have avoided the question that is usually raised first about James' revisions: Didn't he sometimes overwrite to no purpose as a mere occupational disease? Occasionally, without doubt, it is the older James talking instead of a character, as when Pansy, instead of saying, 'I have no voice—just a little thread,' is made to transform this into '. . . just a small sound like the squeak of a slate-pencil making flourishes.' But look at another sample where at first it would appear as though James had taken twice as many words to say the same thing, where 'Marriage meant that a woman should abide with her husband' became 'Marriage meant that a woman should cleave to the man with whom, uttering tremendous vows, she had stood at the altar.' In its context we can at least see what James was after. This passage is part of Isabel's reflections, and both its fuller rhythm and density are meant to increase its *inner* relevance. The best way, therefore, to judge the final value of James' rewriting is to relate it in each case to the character involved, an obligatory proceeding in dealing with the writer who asked, in *The Art of Fiction:* 'What is a picture or a novel that is *not* of character?'

The diverse types of revision demanded by the different characters may also remind us that we have in this book the most interestingly variegated group that James ever created. The center of attention is always Isabel, and the changes devoted to her may be read as a brief outline of the interpretation which James hoped we should give to his heroine. A few involve her looks. Whereas acquaintances of the Archer girls used to refer to her as 'the thin one,' James' tenderness for her was later to make this sound less invidious: 'the willowy one.' From his initial description of her in the house at Albany, he wanted to emphasize that she was less mistress of her fate than she fondly believed. He pointed this up by changing 'young girl' to 'creature of conditions.' He also, as a past master of what could be gained by the specific notation, changed the conditioning of her taste from 'a glimpse of contemporary aesthetics' to 'the music of Gounod, the poetry of Browning, the prose of George Eliot'—a change which recalls that these were also Minny Temple's tastes.

But James' chief interest in his heroine is revealed through another type of change. Warburton's belief that she is 'a thoroughly interesting woman' is made more intimate—'a really interesting little figure.' And a few lines below, when Ralph concludes that a character like hers 'is the finest thing in nature,' he says more precisely what he means by adding, in the revision, that she is 'a real little passionate force.' James devoted many of his later brush strokes to bringing her out as exactly that. Instead of passively wanting 'to be delighted,' she now wants 'to hurl herself into the fray.' It is equally symptomatic of her conduct that she refuses Warburton, not because such a marriage fails 'to correspond to any vision of happiness that she had hitherto entertained,' but because it fails 'to support any enlightened prejudice in favour of the free exploration of life.' The Isabel whom the later James saw with so much lucidity is a daughter of the transcendental afterglow, far less concerned about happiness than about enlightenment and freedom.

Another addition indicates that what is most required to make 'her respond is 'a bait to her imagination.' That is exactly why she is caught by Osmond. Mrs. Touchett originally said that Isabel was capable of marrying him 'for his opinions'; but she heightens this with more of the girl's romanticism in saying 'for the beauty of his opinions or for his autograph of Michael Angelo.' And that is how we see Isabel reacting to him. His 'things of a deep interest' become 'objects, subjects, contacts . . . of a rich association.' She reads into them also, in a favorite phrase of the later James, 'histories within histories.' When she defends him to Ralph, the revision makes her grounds much more explicit by adding to her question, 'What do you know against him?'—'What's the matter with Mr. Osmond's type, if it be one? His being so independent, so individual, is what I most see in him.' And again, instead of saying 'Mr. Osmond is simply a man—he is not a proprietor,' she expands this with her feeling, 'Mr. Osmond's simply a very lonely, a very cultivated and a very honest man—he's not a prodigious proprietor.'

This is the Isabel of whom James felt it no longer adequate just to say, 'she was an excitable creature, and now she was much excited.' He transformed that into an image: 'Vibration was easy to her, was in fact too constant with her, and she found herself now humming like a smitten harp.' Such vibrations are intrinsic to the rhythm of her thought. She no longer reflects merely that 'she had loved him,' but extends that reflection with 'she had so anxiously and yet so ardently given herself.' It is not padding, therefore, when, upon discovering how wrong she has been about Osmond, she does not conclude, 'There was only one way to repair it—to accept it,' but adds '. . . just immensely (oh, with the highest grandeur!) to accept it.'

The revisions affecting Osmond are of a very different sort. Far more of them relate to his appearance, to the polished, elegant and slightly ambiguous surface which James wants the reader to study more fully. His 'sharply-cut face' becomes 'extremely modelled and composed.' James' description of his eyes is far more careful. They are no longer 'luminous' and 'intelligent' expressing 'both softness and keenness,' but 'conscious, curious eyes . . . at once vague and penetrating, intelligent and hard.' This is quite in keeping with his smile, which is now his 'cool' smile, and with his voice, of which it is now said that, though fine, it 'somehow wasn't sweet.' He does not speak 'with feeling' but 'beautifully'; and his laugh, instead of being 'not ill-natured,' has now 'a finer patience.' James has done an expert job of heightening Osmond's thoroughly studied effect. He underscores the fact that Osmond's taste was his only law by saying, not that he lived 'in a serene, impersonal way,' but 'in a sorted, sifted, arranged world,' where his 'superior qualities' become 'standards and touchstones other than the vulgar.'

Osmond is entirely devoted to forms, and to accent this trait, James introduces one of his most interesting later devices: he interrelates Osmond's character with his surroundings in a way that shows again how much the novelist had learned from the plastic arts.[4] On the first occasion that Osmond entertains Isabel, James wants her to be impressed with the rare distinction of the collector's

4 I have given further instances from his earlier works in 'Henry James and the Plastic Arts,' *The Kenyon Review* (Autumn 1943).

villa. Osmond's footboy is now made deliberately picturesque: instead of remaining merely 'the shabby footboy,'
he becomes 'tarnished as to livery and quaint as to type,'
and, with a fine added flourish, James tells us that he
might 'have issued from some stray sketch of old-time manners, been "put in" by the brush of a Longhi or a Goya.'
James also added in the revision that Osmond was marked
for Isabel 'as by one of those signs of the highly curious
that he was showing her on the underside of old plates and
in the corner of sixteenth-century drawings.' As Isabel
thinks over this visit afterwards, she reflects that his care
for beauty 'had been the main occupation of a lifetime of
which the arid places were watered with the sweet sense of
a quaint, half-anxious, half-helpless fatherhood.' In the
revision these thoughts rise from her impression of how she
had seen him: his preoccupation with beauty made his
life 'stretch beneath it in the disposed vistas and with the
ranges of steps and terraces and fountains of a formal Italian garden—allowing only for arid places freshened by the
natural dews,' and so on.

In building up the reasons why she took her romantic
view of him, James also embarked on an extended flight:

What continued to please this young lady was his extraordinary subtlety. There was such a fine intellectual intention in what he said, and the movement of his wit was
like that of a quick-flashing blade.

What continued to please this young woman was that
while he talked so for amusement he didn't talk, as she
had heard people, for 'effect.' He uttered his ideas as if,

odd as they often appeared, he were used to them and had
lived with them; old polished knobs and heads and han-
dles, of precious substance, that could be fitted if necessary
to new walking-sticks—not switches plucked in destitution
from the common tree and then too elegantly waved about.

The new passage stresses, if in oblique ways and with
some needless verbiage, Osmond's utter dependence on art
rather than on nature. The 'old polished knobs,' like the
'complicated medal' to which he is compared, make him
indisseverable from his collector's items. It is not surprising that such a deliberately shaped work of art as he is
'mystified' Isabel. (In the first version he had merely 'puz-
zled' her.) It is fitting too that, as she comes under his fascination, she should feel not merely 'a good deal older
than she had done a year before,' but also 'as if she were
"worth more" for it, like some curious piece in an an-
tiquary's collection.' For, in ways that her inexperience
cannot possibly fathom, that is precisely how Osmond proposes to treat her. She appeals to him, not for being 'as
bright and soft as an April cloud,' but in one of James'
most functional revisions, 'as smooth to his general need
of her as handled ivory to the palm.'

The mystification is only Isabel's, the ambiguity is all
in what Osmond concealed, not in any doubts that James
entertained about him. The revision increases his 'lost'
quality. His 'peculiarities' are called his 'perversities,' and
where it was remarked that he consulted his taste alone,
James now adds 'as a sick man consciously incurable con-
sults at last only his lawyer.' The reader accepts entirely
Ralph's judgment of Osmond as a sterile dilettante; but

his quality is deepened when Ralph recognizes the futility
of trying to persuade Isabel, not that the man is 'a hum-
bug,' but rather that there is something 'sordid or sinister'
in him. With that deepening even Osmond becomes
poignant: his 'keen, expressive, emphatic' face becomes
'firm, refined, slightly ravaged'—a far more telling portrait.

The character in this book around whom ambiguity
gathers most is Madame Merle, since she has to play a double rôle throughout. James' changes involving her are
chiefly of two sorts. He decided, for one thing, that her
surface should be less transparent to Isabel. And so it is
when Isabel asks her if she has not suffered that her 'picturesque smile' is elaborated into 'the amused smile of a
person seated at a game of guesses.' She is also called
'smooth' instead of 'plump.' When Madame Merle introduced her to Osmond, Isabel wondered about 'the nature
of the tie that united them. She was inclined to imagine
that Madame Merle's ties were peculiar.' As James looked
over that, it seemed to strike too close to the actual liaison,
which he didn't want Isabel to suspect for a long time
yet. So he toned it up to 'the nature of the tie binding
these superior spirits. She felt that Madame Merle's ties
always somehow had histories.'

But in the other type of change for Madame Merle,
James felt, as he did with Osmond, that he must make her
character unmistakable to the reader. So he no longer endowed her with 'a certain nobleness,' but with 'a certain
courage'; not with 'geniality' but with 'grace.' Even in
changing the music that Isabel overheard her playing from
'something of Beethoven's' to 'something of Schubert's,'

James must have felt that he was bringing it more within Madame Merle's emotional compass. When Isabel finally comes to know her secret, the girl reflects, not just that her friend was 'false,' but 'even deeply false . . . deeply, deeply, deeply.' And Madame Merle's guilt is spoken of, not in terms 'of vivid proof,' but 'of ugly evidence . . . of grim things produced in court.'

Such details—of which there are many more—are important in allaying the usual suspicion that James' ambiguity is unintentional, the obscurantism of a man who couldn't make up his own mind. When the writing becomes denser, as it frequently does in the revision, this is owing rather to James' gradual development of one of his special gifts, the ability so to handle a conversation that he keeps in the air not merely what is said, but what isn't—the passage of thoughts without words. The situation here which challenged most this skill of the later James was when Warburton turned up again after Isabel's marriage. What she had to decide was whether, despite his honorable pretensions, he was still in love with her. Their interplay is made more subtle. To judge the value of this kind of rewriting you must follow the whole chapter, but one series of slight changes may show what James was about.

As they met again, in the first version, Isabel 'hardly knew whether she were glad or not.' Warburton, however, 'was plainly very well pleased.' In the revision his feelings are not given to us so explicitly: he 'was plainly quite sure of his own sense of the matter.' Only as the conversation advances do Isabel—and the reader—gain the evidence she is after. In a moment or two, he remarks how charming a place she has to live in. In the original he said this,

'brightly, looking about him.' But this became: 'with a
look, round him, at her established home, in which she
might have caught the dim ghost of his old ruefulness.'
That reveals to Isabel nearly all she needs, and her impression is clinched, when, instead of turning upon her
'an eye that gradually became more serious,' he gives her,
in addition, 'the deeper, the deepest consciousness of his
look.' From that moment Isabel knows how unwise it
would be for him to marry her stepdaughter Pansy, no
matter how much Osmond wants the match.

If such a situation caused James thus to weave the texture of his style more complexly, the changes that relate
to Pansy and to Ralph, though equally slight, may reveal
another significant quality. In the scale of emotional vibrations James is more impressive in striking the note of
tenderness than that of passion. We can observe this in
the way he heightened some of his most moving passages.
How utterly Pansy is at the mercy of her father's will is
underlined by several details. Consider, for instance, her
smile, in connection with which we can note again James'
extraordinary care to bring out every revelatory phase of
his characters' looks. At the moment of Pansy's first appearance in the narrative, James remarked that her 'natural and usual expression seemed to be a smile of perfect
sweetness.' But the point about Pansy is that she has had
so little chance to be natural or spontaneous, and so James
revised this: her face was 'painted with a fixed and intensely sweet smile.' So too with the characterizing image
that he created for her. Instead of saying that Pansy entertained Isabel 'like a little lady,' James wrote that she 'rose
to the occasion as the small, winged fairy in the panto-

mime soars by the aid of the dissimulated wire.' Thus
Pansy's trapped state is suggested to us from the outset,
and on the occasion when Isabel tells her that she is going to marry her father, James made two additions that
show how he had learned to handle irony. Originally Isabel had said, 'My good little Pansy, I shall be very kind
to you.' But to that James added: 'A vague, inconsequent
vision of her coming in some odd way to need it had inter-
vened with the effect of a chill.' And when Pansy answered,
'Very well then; I have nothing to fear,' James no longer
had her declare that 'lightly,' but 'with her note of prepared promptitude.' And he also added, as part of Isabel's
reflection: 'What teaching she had had, it seemed to suggest—or what penalties for non-performance she dreaded!'

We can read, in these extensions, the same thing that
we have observed in the major characters, James' deepening of emotional tones. The most affecting passage in the
book is the death of Ralph, for there James is expressing
the tenderness of pure devotion, disencumbered of any
worldly aims. The characterizing image noted above was
designed to increase our sense of Ralph's precarious holds
on life. To increase also our sense of his devotion to Isabel, 'his cousin' was twice changed to 'the person in the
world in whom he was most interested.' The scene between
these two, as he lies dying, is very short, and the only significant change is in Ralph's last speech. In the original
this read: ' "And remember this," he continued, "that if
you have been hated, you have also been loved." ' To that
James added: ' "Ah, but, Isabel—*adored!*" he just audibly
and lingeringly breathed.' There it may become a debatable matter of taste whether the simpler form is not

more moving; but the later James felt impelled to a more high-keyed emotional register. Both Ralph and Isabel, instead of 'murmuring' or 'adding softly' are made to 'wail.' [5] It is difficult to keep such tones from becoming sentimental, but how little James was inclined to sentimentalize can be seen in his handling of Ralph's funeral. Originally James pronounced it 'not a disagreeable one'; but he made his later statement stronger: it was 'neither a harsh nor a heavy one.'

IV

The two most extensive passages of rewriting are yet to be looked at. One relates to the Countess Gemini, and the other to Caspar Goodwood. Both can give us insight into how James conceived dramatic structure, and how he also felt that the climax of this book needed strengthening.

In comparing the two versions, it is notable that the sequence of chapters which James pronounced, in the preface, as being the best in the book—the sequence that extends from Isabel's glimpse of the two together, with Osmond seated while Madame Merle is standing, through the long vigil in which Isabel gradually pieces together her situation—that these three chapters (XL-XLII), with their important issues, were left substantially unchanged. So too with

[5] This is also true in the other most directly emotional scene, the death of Ralph's father:

' "My father died an hour ago."

"Ah, my poor Ralph!" the girl murmured, putting out her hand to him.'

' "My dear father died an hour ago."

"Ah, my poor Ralph!" she gently wailed, putting out her two hands to him.'

the fateful interview between Osmond and Isabel (Chapter XLVI) which shows how hopelessly far apart they have grown. But the scene with the Countess (Chapter LI), in which Isabel's suspicions are first given explicit names, was greatly recast. Some of the reasons for this are suggested by what James wrote in his notebook at the time when the novel had begun to appear in *The Atlantic* and he was trying to see his way clear to his conclusion: 'After Isabel's marriage there are five more instalments, and the success of the whole story greatly depends upon this portion being well conducted or not. Let me then make the most of it—let me imagine the best. There has been a want of action in the earlier part, and it may be made up here. The elements that remain are in themselves, I think, very interesting, and they are only to be strongly and happily combined. The weakness of the whole story is that it is too exclusively psychological—that it depends too little on incident; but the complete unfolding of the situation that is established by Isabel's marriage may nonetheless be quite sufficiently dramatic. The idea of the whole thing is that the poor girl, who has dreamed of freedom and nobleness, who has done, as she believes, a generous, natural, clear-sighted thing, finds herself in reality ground in the very mill of the conventional. After a year or two of marriage the antagonism between her nature and Osmond's comes out—the open opposition of a noble character and a narrow one. There is a great deal to do here in a small compass; every word, therefore, must tell—every touch must count. If the last five parts of the story appear crowded, this will be rather a good defect in consideration of the perhaps too great diffuseness of the earlier portion.'

As James went on outlining his intentions, he was still undecided whether the revelation of Pansy's parentage should come through Madame Merle herself or through the Countess: 'Better on many grounds that it should be the latter; and yet in that way I lose the "great scene" between Madame Merle and Isabel.' Twenty-five years later he was still bothered by what he had lost. In the passage of deadly quietness between Isabel and Osmond, and, subsequently, between Isabel and Madame Merle, he seems to have felt that his drama was too inward, that he needed a more emotional scene. And so he rewrote nearly all the lines in which the Countess told Isabel of the liaison.

He had already given considerable attention to making the Countess' character a more lively mixture. Ralph's first description of her was changed from 'rather wicked' to 'rather impossible'; and in her own disarming self-charac-terization, instead of saying, 'I am only rather light,' she pronounced herself 'only rather an idiot and a bore.' James had originally said that her expression was 'by no means disagreeable'; but here he particularized: it was made up of 'various intensities of emphasis and wonder, of horror and joy.' Also, to a quite astonishing degree, by recurring to a bird-image for her, he sustained her in a whir. For example, in her first meeting with Isabel, she delivered her remarks 'with a variety of little jerks and glances.' But the bird-motif gave these the momentum of 'little jerks and pecks, of roulades of shrillness,' with the result that James was stimulated to a further flight of his own, and added that her accent was 'as some fond recall of good English, or rather of good American, in adversity.'

This kind of a character had dramatic possibilities, and, in his revision, James exploited them to the full. He did everything he could to make her revelations to Isabel into the 'great scene' he had missed. Isabel is alone, thinking of what will happen if, in defiance of Osmond's wishes, she goes to England to see Ralph before he dies. Then, suddenly, the Countess 'stood before her.' Thus the original, but in the rewriting the Countess 'hovered before her.' And to give us an intimation that something is coming, James added that the Countess 'lived assuredly, it might be said, at the window of her spirit, but now she was leaning far out.' As Lawrence Leighton, who first drew my attention to the importance of this scene for James' structure, remarked, this is like 'an extra blast from the trumpets' to announce the herald. It occurs to Isabel for the first time that her sister-in-law might say something, not 'important,' but 'really human.'

In what follows much subtle attention was paid to the Countess' diction. James endowed her with a more characteristic colloquial patter, with such epithets as 'poverina' and 'cara mia.' Instead of saying that Madame Merle had wanted 'to save her reputation,' she says, 'to save her skin'; and, in her view, Isabel has not merely 'such a pure mind' —she calls it 'beastly pure,' as such a woman would. Her speeches are considerably increased in length, one of them by almost a page. There is hardly any addition to her ideas, but as Mr. Leighton also observed, 'James wanted a good harangue, the sort of speech an actress could get her teeth into.' Her quality is melodramatic, but it is effectively more baleful than in the first version.

James has also built up the contrast between her and Isabel. The Countess expected—and hoped—that the girl would burst out with a denunciation of Osmond. But instead she is filled with pity for Madame Merle. She thinks even of Osmond's first wife, that 'he must have been false' to her—'and so very soon!' That last phrase is an addition that emphasizes Isabel's incurable innocence, despite all the experience through which she is passing. It glances ironically also at her own situation. When she goes on to reflect that at least Osmond has been faithful to her, the Countess says it depends on what you call faithful: 'When he married you he was no longer the lover of another woman—*such* a lover as he had been, *cara mia,* between their risks and their precautions, while the thing lasted!' Everything after the dash is added, and we can hear the Countess smacking her lips over such details, while Isabel recoils into herself. Where the first version had remarked that she 'hesitated, though there was a question in her eyes,' the utter cleavage between her and her gossipy interlocutress is now brought out: she 'hesitated as if she had not heard; as if her question—though it was sufficiently there in her eyes—were all for herself.' When, a moment or two later, Isabel wondered why Madame Merle never wanted to marry Osmond, the Countess had originally contented herself with saying that Madame Merle 'had grown more ambitious.' But to that James added: ' "besides, she has never had, about him," the Countess went on, leaving Isabel to wince for it so tragically afterwards—"she *had* never had, what you might call any illusions of *intelli*-

gence."' The Countess is happy to get in a dig at her
brother, but for Isabel and for the reader there is the irony
that Isabel herself had been fooled by just such illusions.
That gives the final twist to the knife.

After this scene there remain only four chapters. There
is the brief final encounter with Madame Merle, who sees
in an instant that Isabel now knows everything. Isabel then
says good-bye to Pansy, but promises that she won't desert
her. The rest of the book is taken up with Isabel's trip to
England, with her farewell to Ralph, and with Caspar's
return to her. The last chapter is largely her struggle with
him, and James' significant additions are led up to by the
emphases that he has given to Caspar's character earlier
in the book. He has introduced many details that sharpen
the impression of Caspar's indomitable energy. When Isabel first compares him with Warburton, she feels that there
is 'something too forcible, something oppressive and re-
strictive' about him. But this was made more concrete: 'a
disagreeably strong push, a kind of hardness of presence.'
A revelatory image was introduced to contrast Isabel's feeling about Warburton: instead of refusing to 'lend a re-
ceptive ear' to his suit, she now 'resists conquest' at his
'large quiet hands.' But Caspar is 'a kind of fate,' now,
indeed, 'a kind of grim fate.' He himself gives fuller expression to the tension between them when he has first
pursued her to London. Instead of saying, 'Apparently it
was disagreeable to you even to write,' he makes it 'repug-
nant.' And he remarks bitterly, not that his insistence on
his suit 'displeases' her, but that it 'disgusts.' As the best
means of characterizing him, James developed a recurrent
image of armor. In his first account he had merely re-

marked that Caspar was 'the strongest man' Isabel had ever known; but to this he added: 'she saw the different fitted parts of him as she had seen, in museums and portraits, the different fitted parts of armoured warriors—in plates of steel handsomely inlaid with gold.' Later on, his eyes, instead of wearing 'an expression of ardent remonstrance,' seemed 'to shine through the vizard of a helmet.' And when Isabel tries to measure his possible suffering, she no longer reflects that 'he had a sound constitution,' but that 'he was naturally plated and steeled, armed essentially for aggression.'

He follows her to Italy to object strenuously to her engagement to Osmond: 'Where does he come from? Where does he belong?' That second question was added in the revision, as was also Isabel's thought, 'She had never been so little pleased with the way he said "belawng." ' But, in spite of everything, Isabel cannot escape feeling Caspar's power; and in rewriting their final scene, James made an incisive analysis of his mixed repulsion and attraction for her. She is alone under the trees at Gardencourt, when Caspar suddenly appears—just as Warburton had surprised her there once before. In what follows we are made to feel her overpowering sensation of his physical presence, from the moment that James adds that he was 'beside her on the bench and pressingly turned to her.' As he insists that her husband is 'the deadliest of fiends,' and that he, Caspar, is determined to prevent her from the 'horror' of returning to him (both 'deadliest' and 'horror' were additions), Isabel realizes that 'she had never been loved before.' To that realization the original had added: 'It wrapped her about; it lifted her off her feet.' But now James wrote: 'She had believed it, but this was different; this was the hot wind of the desert, at the approach of which the others dropped dead, like mere sweet airs of the garden. It wrapped her about; it lifted her off her feet, while the very taste of it, as of something potent, acrid, and strange, forced open her set teeth.'

That image takes her as far away from her surroundings and the gentlemanly devotion of a Warburton as it does from the decadent egotism of an Osmond. For a moment she is completely overpowered. Caspar's voice, saying, 'Be mine, as I'm yours,' comes to her, not merely 'through a confusion of sound,' but 'harsh and terrible, through a confusion of vaguer sounds.' He takes her in his arms, and, in the first version, the climax is reached with: 'His kiss was like a flash of lightning; when it was dark again she was free.' But now James felt it necessary to say far more: 'His kiss was like white lightning, a flash that spread, and spread again, and stayed; and it was extraordinary as if, while she took it, she felt each thing in his hard manhood that had least pleased her, each aggressive fact of his face, his figure, his presence, justified of its intense identity and made one with this act of possession. So had she heard of those wrecked and under water following a train of images before they sink. But when darkness returned she was free.'

That conveys James' awareness of how Isabel, in spite of her marriage, has remained essentially virginal, and of how her resistance and her flight from Caspar are partly fear of sexual possession. But the fierce attraction she also feels in this passage would inevitably operate likewise for a girl of her temperament, in making her do what she con-

ceived to be her duty, and sending her back to her husband.

V

That brings us to the ending of the book, which has sel-
dom been rightly interpreted. The difference between the
two versions is one of the few of James' revisions that is
generally known. Henrietta has told Caspar that Isabel has
gone back to Rome:

'Look here, Mr. Goodwood,' she said; 'just you wait.' On
which he looked up at her.

Thus the final lines in the original. But to these James
added:

—but only to guess, from her face, with a revulsion, that
she simply meant he was young. She stood shining at him
with that cheap comfort, and it added, on the spot, thirty
years to his life. She walked him away with her, however,
as if she had given him now the key to patience.

Many critics have held this difference to mean that James
had changed his mind, that in the original he had given
Caspar more hope. But he seems rather to have made unmistakably explicit what he had always intended to imply.
He had said in his notebook outline that Isabel was to be
greatly moved by Caspar's 'passionate outbreak': 'she feels
the full force of his devotion—to which she has never done
justice; but she refuses. She starts again for Italy—and her
departure is the climax and termination of the story.'

James had also observed there that Henrietta was to have 'the last word,' to utter 'a characteristic characterization of Isabel.' But he must have felt in revising that he had been too brief, that he had failed to drive home to the reader that what was being expressed was no sure promise about Isabel, but rather Henrietta's optimism, which refuses to accept defeat.

The end of Isabel's career is not yet in sight. That fact raises a critical issue about James' way of rounding off his narratives. He was keenly aware of what his method involved. As he wrote in his notebook, upon concluding his detailed project: 'With strong handling it seems to me that it may all be very true, very powerful, very touching. The obvious criticism of course will be that it is not finished—that it has not seen the heroine to the end of her situation —that I have left her *en l'air*. This is both true and false. The *whole* of anything is never told; you can only take what groups together. What I have done has that unity—it groups together. It is complete in itself—and the rest may be taken up or not, later.'

This throws a great deal of light—perhaps more than any single passage of his published work—on how James conceived of structure. He recounted in the preface to the *Portrait* how Turgenieff had encouraged him in his belief that the important thing to start with was not an air-tight plot, but rather a character or group of characters who are so living that the main question becomes to 'invent and select' the complications that such characters 'would be most likely to produce and to feel.'

Years before the *Portrait,* William James had commented on the effect of such a method, as it struck him in *A Most*

Extraordinary Case (1868), one of the first half dozen
stories that Henry had printed. William felt that here he
understood for the first time what Henry was aiming for:
'to give an impression like that we often get of people in
life: Their orbits come out of space and lay themselves for
a short time along of ours, and then off they whirl again
into the unknown, leaving us with little more than an impression of their reality and a feeling of baffled curiosity as
to the mystery of the beginning and the end of their being.'
William thought such a method difficult to make succeed,
but 'with a deep justification in nature.' He was to grow
somewhat less sure of its efficacy, as can be read in his tone
about *The Tragic Muse:* 'the final winding up is, as
usual with you, rather a losing of the story in the sand,
yet that is the way in which things lose themselves in real
life.' Henry, on the other hand, grew steadily to have more
confidence in what he was doing, until he declared, in the
preface to *Roderick Hudson:* 'Really, universally, relations stop nowhere, and the exquisite problem of the
artist is eternally but to draw, by a geometry of his own,
the circle within which they shall happily *appear* to do so.'
That gives his essential conception of the kind of wholeness
that form imposes.

He had been particularly concerned in the *Portrait* with
launching Isabel Archer into action, with presenting her
so vividly that his narrative would compose itself around
the primary question, 'Well, what will she *do?*' It has recently been assumed that James believed entirely in the
rightness of his heroine's conduct, and that since our age
no longer feels as he—and she—did about the strictness of
the marriage vow, we can no longer respond to the book

except as to a period piece. But that is to misread not merely the ending, but all of James' own 'characteristic characterization' of Isabel. He could hardly have made a more lucid summary of the weaknesses that she exposed to Europe: 'her meagre knowledge, her inflated ideals, her confidence at once innocent and dogmatic, her temper at once exacting and indulgent'—that whole passage of analysis on the evening after her arrival at Gardencourt, a passage untouched in the revision, is meant to have our closest scrutiny.

As Isabel embarks on her 'free exploration' of life, Henrietta is outspoken in declaring that she is drifting rather to 'some great mistake,' that she is not enough 'in contact with reality,' with the 'toiling, striving' world. Ralph tells her that she has 'too much conscience'—a peculiarly American complication in the romantic temperament. Although all her diverse friends are united in their disapproval of Osmond, she proceeds to do the wrong thing for the right reasons. She has a special pride in marrying him, since she feels that she is not only 'taking,' but also 'giving'; she feels too the release of transferring some of the burden of her inheritance to another's conscience—James' way of commenting on how harm was done to her by her money. But once she discerns what Osmond is really like, and how he has trapped her, she is by no means supine in his toils. She stands up to him with dignity, she even asks Pansy, 'Will you come away with me now?' Yet Isabel knows that is impossible; she knows, even as she leaves, that she will have to return to Rome for Pansy's sake.

But much more is involved than that—James' whole conception of the discipline of suffering. It is notable that his kinship here to Hawthorne becomes far more palpable in the final version. Take the instance when, at the time of Ralph's death, Isabel realizes how Mrs. Touchett has missed the essence of life by her inability to feel. It seemed to Isabel that Ralph's mother 'would find it a blessing to-day to be able to indulge a regret. She wondered whether Mrs. Touchett were not trying, whether she had not a desire for the recreation of grief.' James made this much fuller, particularly the latter portion. Isabel wondered if Mrs. Touchett 'were not even missing those enrichments of consciousness and privately trying—reaching out for some aftertaste of life, dregs of the banquet; the testimony of pain or the cold recreation of remorse.' The view of suffering adumbrated there, even the phrasing, recalls Hawthorne's *The Christmas Banquet*, where the most miserable fate is that of the man whose inability to feel bars him out even from the common bond of woe.

The common bond of sin, so central to Hawthorne's thought, was also accentuated through James' retouching. When Madame Merle finally foresees what is ahead, she says to Osmond in the original, 'How do bad people end? You have made me bad.' But James extended this with a new italicized emphasis, 'How do bad people end?—especially as to their *common* crimes. You have made me as bad as yourself.' Isabel's link with humanity, if not through sin —unless her willful spirit counts as such—is through her acceptance of suffering. The inevitability of her lot is made more binding in the revision. Her reflection that 'she should not escape, she should last,' becomes 'she should never escape, she should last to the end.' She takes on heightened stature when James no longer says that, while

she sat with Ralph, 'her spirit rose,' but that 'her ache for
herself became somehow her ache for *him.*' The pathos of
her situation is also intensified in proportion to her greater
knowledge of what is involved. 'She reflected that things
change but little, while people change so much' is far less
affecting than 'she envied the security of valuable "pieces"
which change by no hair's breadth, only grow in value,
while their owners lose inch by inch, youth, happiness,
beauty.'

In both the original and the revision Isabel lays the
most scrupulous emphasis upon the sacredness of a promise. Despite all her eagerness for culture, hers is no specu-
lative spirit. Osmond comes to despise her for having 'the
moral horizon' of a Unitarian minister—'poor Isabel, who
had never been able to understand Unitarianism!' But
whether she understands it or not, she is a firm grand-
daughter of the Puritans, not in her thought but in her
moral integrity. In portraying her character and her fate,
James was also writing an essay on the interplay of free will
and determinism. Isabel's own view is that she was 'perfectly free,' that she married Osmond of her most deliberate
choice, and that, however miserable one may be, one must
accept the consequences of one's acts. James knew how
little she was free, other than to follow to an impulsive
extreme everything she had been made by her environment
and background.

Thus he leaves her to confront her future, and is satisfied if he has endowed his characters with so much 'felt life'
that the reader must weigh for himself what is likely to lie
ahead in her relation with Osmond. It may be that, as
Isabel herself conjectures, he may finally 'take her money

and let her go.' It may be that once she has found a husband for Pansy, she will feel that she no longer has to remain in Rome. James believed that the arbitrary circle of
art should stimulate such speculations beyond its confines,
and thus create also the illusion of wider life. He had
about Isabel a tragic sense, but he did not write a tragedy,
as he was to do in *The Wings of the Dove,* since this earlier
drama was lacking in the finality of purgation and judgment. But his view of his material was not at all ambiguous. He knew how romantic Isabel was, how little experienced she was in mature social behavior. He had shown
that she was completely mistaken in believing that 'the
world lay before her—she could do whatever she chose.'
But James also knew the meaning and the value of renunciation. The American life of his day, in its reckless plunge
to outer expansiveness and inner defeat, had taught him
that as his leading spiritual theme. Through Isabel Archer
he gave one of his fullest and freshest expressions of inner
reliance in the face of adversity. It is no wonder that, after
enumerating her weaknesses, he had concluded: 'she would
be an easy victim of scientific criticism if she were not intended to awaken on the reader's part an impulse more
tender . . .'

Index